D0899116

Culture

Culture
Terry Eagleton

YALE UNIVERSITY PRESS
NEW HAVEN AND LONDON

For information about this and other Yale University Press publications, please contact:
U.S. Office: sales.press@yale.edu   yalebooks.com
Europe Office: sales@yaleup.co.uk   yalebooks.co.uk

Typeset in Adobe Garamond Pro by IDSUK (DataConnection) Ltd
Printed in the United States of America

Library of Congress Cataloging-in-publication Data

Eagleton, Terry, 1943–
Culture / Terry Eagleton.
New Haven, CT : Yale University, 2016. | Includes
    bibliographical references and index.
LCCN 2015037500 | ISBN 9780300218794 (alk. paper)
Culture. | Civilization, Modern.
HM621. E154 2016 | DDC 306—dc23
LC record available at http://lccn.loc.gov/2015037500

A catalogue record for this book is available from the British Library.

10 9 8 7 6 5 4 3 2 1

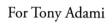

For Tony Adami

Contents

Preface

CULTURE IS A MULTIFACETED concept, which makes it hard to run a tightly unified case about it. This book accordingly sacrifices any strict unity of argument in order to approach its subject from a number of different perspectives. I begin by examining various senses of the term 'culture', and go on to explore some key differences between the idea of culture and the notion of civilisation. I then go on to examine the postmodern doctrine of culturalism, for which culture is fundamental to human existence, and in doing so submit the concepts of diversity, plurality, hybridity and inclusivity to some unfashionable criticism. I also take issue with the tenets of cultural relativism.

Culture can be seen as a kind of social unconscious, and with this idea in mind I look at the work of two major exponents of it: the political philosopher Edmund Burke, an author whose writings are widely known but who is not commonly associated with the idea of culture; and the German philosopher Johann Gottfried Herder, whose extraordinarily original thinking on cultural questions is not as much in vogue as it should be. I also have some comments on culture as the social unconscious in the work of T.S. Eliot and Raymond Williams – two thinkers for whom culture is an utterly vital concept, but from sharply opposed political standpoints.

A chapter on Oscar Wilde pays homage to this most audacious and agreeable of cultural critics, while also summarising some of the versions of culture examined so far. I then turn to the question of why the idea of culture has bulked so large in what is often seen as a philistine modern age, and set out a range of reasons for this. Chief among them are the idea of culture as an aesthetic or utopian critique of industrial capitalism; the rise of revolutionary nationalism, multiculturalism and identity politics; the search for a substitute for religion; and the emergence of the so-called culture industry. I also take a critical look at the doctrine of culturalism, for which culture goes all the way down in human existence, as well as at the question of cultural relativism. A Conclusion lays out a number of reasons for deciding that culture is by no means as central to modern societies as some of its apologists would imagine.

Perspicacious readers will note that there is an Irish motif running throughout the book, from Swift, Burke and Wilde to Irish anti-colonial politics.

T.E.

CHAPTER ONE

Culture and Civilisation

'CULTURE' IS AN exceptionally complex word – the second or third most complex word in the English language, so it has been claimed[1] – but four major senses of it stand out. It can mean (1) a body of artistic and intellectual work; (2) a process of spiritual and intellectual development; (3) the values, customs, beliefs and symbolic practices by which men and women live; or (4) a whole way of life. 'Lappish culture' can mean the poetry, music and dance of the Lapps; or it can include the kind of food they eat, the sort of sport they play and the type of religion they practise; or it can stretch even further to cover Lappish society as a whole, taking in its transport network, system of voting and methods of garbage disposal. In all these cases, what may be typical of Lappish culture may not be peculiar to it. The Lapps, for example, eat reindeer, but so do other peoples. They are required by law to have snow tyres on their cars in winter, but this is also true of some other northerly nations. You can, however, visit Santa Claus at his home on the Arctic Circle the whole year round in Lapland, a treat which probably can't be found anywhere else on the planet.

Culture in the artistic and intellectual sense of the word may well involve innovation, whereas culture as a way of life is generally a question of habit. You can compose a new concerto or publish a new journal, but when it comes to culture in the broader sense of the word, the idea of a new cultural event has a mildly self-contradictory ring to it, though such things do of course exist. Culture in this sense is what you have done before – even, perhaps, what your ancestors have done millions of times over. For your own conduct to be valid, it may need to be in line with theirs. Culture in the sense of art can be avant-garde, while culture as a way of life is mostly a matter of custom. Since artistic culture is often a minority affair – including, as it does, work which is not easy of access – it differs in this respect from culture as a process of development, which one might see as a more egalitarian matter. If those who are uncultured now may become cultivated later, then it may be that anyone can accumulate cultural capital if only they put their mind to it. You can tend your own spiritual growth over the years, rather as agriculture involves the tending of natural growth over a period of time. Culture in this sense is not something you acquire all at once, like a puppy or a bout of influenza.

Generally speaking, the first three meanings of the word would seem more useful than the fourth (culture as a whole way of life), which is at risk of taking in too much. Raymond Williams remarks that 'the difficulty about the idea of culture is that we are continually forced to extend it, until it becomes almost identical with our whole common life'.[2] Quite why we are 'forced' to extend the word isn't clear, but Williams is surely right to see that the term 'culture' has certain built-in inflationary tendencies. They do not seem to worry him, however, as much as they should. If the aesthetic sense of the word may be too narrow, the anthropological sense can be too amorphous. Even so, the more expansive meaning has its uses. Williams himself illustrates the difference between culture as art and culture as way of life by pointing out that the culture of the British working-class movement is not so much a question of painting and poetry as a matter of political institutions: trade unions, the cooperative movement, the Labour Party and the like. For the German philosopher Johann Gottfried Herder, whose work we shall be looking at later, culture includes industry, commerce and technology quite as much as values and sentiments.

In his *Notes Towards the Definition of Culture*, T.S. Eliot takes culture to include 'all the characteristic activities and interests of a people', and goes on to list a number of stereotypically English examples: Derby Day, Henley Regatta, the dart board, Wensleydale cheese, Gothic churches, boiled cabbage, beetroot in vinegar, the music of Elgar and so on.[3] Commenting on this somewhat whimsical selection of national treasures, Raymond Williams notes that far from representing the typical activities of a people, Eliot's inventory really boils down to 'sport, food and a little art', which suggests an older, more exclusive notion of cultivation. Wouldn't the characteristic activities of the English, Williams inquires, include steelmaking, the stock exchange, mixed farming and London Transport as well?[4] Eliot, in other words, takes himself to be describing culture as a whole way of life (definition 4 above), but is in fact restricting the notion to customs and symbolic practices (definition 3). There is, then, an immediate problem: does the culture of a people include its practical, material mode of existence, or should it be confined to the symbolic sphere?

Perhaps it is not too pedantic to make a distinction here between Lappish culture and Lappish civilisation. Painting, cuisine and attitudes to sexuality in Lapland would come under the former, while transport systems and forms of central heating would fall under the latter. 'Culture' and 'civilisation' originally meant much the same thing; but in the modern age, as we shall see, they have not only been distinguished but actually viewed as opposites. In the annals of modern history, the Germans have generally been seen as representing culture, while the French win first prize as flagbearers of civilisation. The Germans have Goethe, Kant and

Mendelssohn, while the French have perfume, haute cuisine and Châteauneuf-du-Pape. The Germans are spiritual while the French are sophisticated. It is a choice between Wagner and Dior. Stereotypically speaking, the former are too high-minded and the latter too hard-boiled.

Roughly speaking, mailboxes are part of civilisation, but what colour you paint them (green in the Republic of Ireland, for example) is a matter of culture. You need traffic lights in modern societies, but red does not have to signal 'Stop' and green 'Go'. During the Cultural Revolution in Beijing there was a demand for it to be the other way round. A good deal of culture involves less what you do than how you do it. It can denote a set of styles, techniques and established procedures. There are different ways of running a car plant, for example, which is why one can contrast Renault culture with Volkswagen culture. Everyone has relatives, but whether tradition ordains that your dealings with some of them must habitually involve joking is a cultural affair. 'Police culture' includes not so much truncheons and rubber bullets as the readiness of some police forces to deploy them at the slightest provocation. It covers the customary ways the police think and behave – how they feel about rapists, for example, or whether junior officers salute senior ones. Australian culture probably doesn't include the fact that there are a number of car rental facilities in Alice Springs, but it does cover barbecues, Rules football and spending time on the beach. British culture ranges from irony and understatement to sporting red plastic noses at the slightest opportunity.

There are times when the term 'culture' may seem super-fluous. To claim that there is a pervasive culture of match-fixing in football is to claim that there is a good deal of match-fixing in football. To call it a culture, however, implies that it is habitual, well-entrenched, perhaps taken for granted and governed by certain established procedures. Culture in this sense may seem a purely descriptive category, but this can be deceptive. To see one's way of life as distinctive, for example, generally involves some sense of how it differs from other people's, and thus perhaps a degree of suspicion of them. Most forms of collective identity depend on the exclusion of others, sometimes necessarily so. You cannot be a member of the Royal College of Nurses if you are a professional sword swallower. Sometimes the exclusions are less innocent. There would be no need for Northern Irish Unionists to fly St George's flags were there not hordes of Catholic nationalists ensconced across the street. The apparently innocuous idea of culture may thus contain the seeds of discord from the outset. Besides, what may look like a purely factual description from one viewpoint – 'the culture of the landowning gentry', let us say – may not be so from another (that of those who till their fields, for example).

The notion of culture as a whole way of life probably works better with tribal or premodern societies than it does with modern ones. In fact, the study of premodern peoples is one of the sources from which it derives. This is not because such societies constitute organic wholes. There are no 'whole' societies, in the sense of societies absolved from conflict and contradiction. It is rather because it may be harder in premodern conditions to draw a clear line between symbolic practices on the one hand and social or economic activities on the other. To include, say, work and politics under the heading of culture when one is dealing with the Dinka probably makes more sense than it does when one is speaking of the Danes. In premodern times, the practical and the symbolic are likely to be more closely allied than they are in the modern age. Tribal peoples, for example, do not tend to think of their labour and commerce as constituting an autonomous region known as the economy, entirely distinct from spiritual beliefs and time-honoured duties. In the modern world, by contrast, the economic ceases to pay much heed to time-hallowed rights and customs. Your boss no longer feels morally obliged to take a paternalist interest in your general welfare, or at least to make a passable show of doing so. You now work simply to stay alive or purely to make a profit, not (in addition) to pay homage to the Almighty, fulfil your customary obligations to your feudal lord or play your allotted part in the tribe's kinship system. Social facts begin to come adrift from cultural values, a process that involves new kinds of freedom as well as new forms of hardship. You can now sell your labour to the highest bidder, for example, rather than being bound hand and foot to a single master. Power can no longer easily cloak itself in spiritual authority. You are less likely to feel constrained by the subtly coercive force of tradition, and can be relieved of the tedious necessity to banter with your nephew every time you clap eyes on him.

Take the difference between a nineteenth-century peasant and a modern factory worker. On the traditional family smallholding, labour and domestic life are more closely inter-woven than they are in a mill town, where the industrial is one thing and the domestic another. Peasants have children, for example, for much the same reasons that anyone else does, but also because they will grow up to work on the land, take care of you in your old age and eventually inherit one's modest allocation of acres. As well as looking cute, children represent labour-power, a welfare system and the continued survival of the farm. In modern civilisation, by contrast, it is hard to say what children are for. They don't work, for example, and some of them are not particularly decorative. They are expen-sive to keep and not always rational. Caring for them as infants is one of the most arduous forms of labour known to humankind. Given all this, it is surprising that the modern human species manages to reproduce itself at all. Yet there is no question of the utility of children among peasants and tenant farmers.

Who you marry in such conditions may also be partly governed by economic factors, which means that there is less of a sharp distinction between sexuality and property than there is in small-town Ohio. Sexuality may be less a matter of soft music and candle-lit dinners than of dowries and match-makers. In fact, a sizeable sector of the population will probably be fortunate to have dinners at all, candle-lit or otherwise. If this interlocking of the sexual and economic marks the lower orders in rural society, it is also a feature of the land-owning gentry and aristocracy. Upper-class marriages, for example, may involve the consolidation of two great estates, as with the union of Tom Jones and Sophia Western at the end of Henry Fielding's novel *Tom Jones*; or they may establish a mutually beneficial alliance between landed and indus-trial capital.

There are circumstances, then, in which it may make sense to extend the word 'culture' to social existence as a whole, as long as one does so without nostalgia. It should not be taken to suggest, for example, that everyday life in pre-industrial Britain was qualitatively finer than it is in modern-day Chicago. On the contrary, it was in many respects a great deal worse. Nor should it be taken to idealise tribal societies. On purely descriptive grounds, however, 'Tuareg culture' can probably include certain everyday social activities with less of a strain than 'Texan culture'. It is hard to think of drilling oil-wells or keeping a Kalashnikov under your bed as belonging to the cultural domain. There is another issue at stake here as well. A good deal of what goes on in industrialised societies is

9

thought to be non-cultural in the sense of not being conspicuously valuable. Coal mines and cotton mills belong to the realm of material necessity, not to the sphere of spiritual freedom. They are non-cultural in a normative as well as a descriptive sense, meaning that the quality of life they involve leaves a good deal to be desired. This, to be sure, applies even more flagrantly to most pre-industrial forms of labour. What emerges with the Industrial Revolution, however, is an impassioned revolt against civilisation as such, which now appears spiritually bankrupt as a whole. This, at any rate, is the view of such jaundiced observers as Friedrich Schiller, John Ruskin and William Morris. It is also the opinion of D.H. Lawrence, who writes of industrial England as involving 'the utter negation of natural beauty, the utter negation of the gladness of life, the utter absence of the instinct for shapely beauty which every bird and beast has'.[5] Civilisation is now a matter of fact, while culture is a question of value. In this sense of the term, culture now appears to lie irretrievably in the past. It is the paradise we have lost, the happy garden from which we have been rudely ejected, the organic society that has always just disappeared over the historical horizon.

It is industrial civilisation, then, which helps to bring the idea of culture to birth. The word 'culture' did not become widely current until the nineteenth century. The more everyday experience seems soulless and impoverished, the more an ideal of culture is promoted by way of contrast. The more crassly materialistic civilisation grows, the more exalted and other-worldly culture appears. Middle-class citizens of Berlin and Vienna began to dream of the unblemished organic society of ancient Greece. Culture and civilisation now seemed to be at loggerheads. The former is a Romantic concept, while the latter belongs to the language of Enlightenment.

Yet civilisation is not the only antithesis of culture. There is also a polarity between culture and barbarism. In fact, for some thinkers these two contrasts come to more or less the same thing. Does this mean that much of what passes for civilised existence is essentially barbaric? There are certainly those who have believed so. If the arts, along with moral values and spiritual truths, represents what is finest in human living, then on this view much of our existence is not really human at all. Yet while culture in this sense of the word stands as a rebuke to everyday life, culture in the sense of symbolic practice is stitched into it at every point. You cannot run a pig farm or an army camp without culture – not in the sense of piping Mahler into the pigsties or distributing copies of Diderot among the ranks, but in the sense of dealing in values and significations. You can see culture as a specific sector of civilisation, from brass bands and kindergartens to fashion shows and basilicas; but it also signifies the symbolic dimension of society as a whole, permeating it from one end to another, as omnipresent as the Almighty. There can be no distinctively human activity without signs and values. In any case, though art may find itself at odds with social institutions, it is a social institution in itself, and can survive only with the aid of other such set-ups. If you want novels, you need paper mills and printing presses. Civilisation is the precondition of culture. Samuel Taylor Coleridge speaks in *On the Constitution of Church and State* of culture in the sense of moral well-being as being the more fundamental of the two, but the truth is that culture is the creature of the very civilisation to which it seeks to lend some spiritual foundation.

It may seem that culture is a question of value and civilisation a matter of fact, yet each term can be used in both normative and descriptive ways. The word 'whole', in the phrase 'a whole way of life', can mean (descriptively) 'entire', but also (normatively) 'unified', 'integral', 'without deficiency'. When the nineteenth-century anthropologist Edward Burnett Tylor defines both culture and civilisation as 'that complex whole which includes knowledge, belief, art, morals, law, custom, and any other capabilities and habits acquired by man as a member of society', he is speaking descriptively.[6] When the eighteenth-century poet Henry James Pye declares in his poem 'The Progress of Refinement' that 'The sable African no culture boasts', he intends the comment as evaluative. He means that Africans have culture in the sense of a form of life, but not in the sense of fine living. They have a way of life, but it is worthless. Mahatma Gandhi's legendary gibe when asked what he thought of British civilisation – 'I think it would be a good idea' – turns on a mischievous slide from civilisation-as-fact to civilisation-as-value. In one sense, it is not civilised behaviour to torture, but in another sense it is, since a good many civilisations engage in it. Only civilised people can place sticks of gelignite in children's playgrounds. The work of T.S. Eliot, whose views on culture we shall be considering later, is exemplary of these ambiguities. Eliot sometimes uses the word descriptively, to mean 'the way of life of a particular people living together in one place'.[7] This is not the most astute of formulations, since British culture, for example, is made up nowadays of different peoples living in different ways in the same place, as well as the lifestyle of some Britons who live abroad. But it is also at odds with Eliot's normative use of the term, as when he speaks of culture as 'that which makes life worth living'.[8] Culture in his view is sometimes a matter of manners, religion, the arts and ideas, and sometimes 'that which makes [a society] a society', which must surely include more than chapels and concert halls.[9] To compound the confusion, he also writes of a future 'of which it is possible to say that it will have no culture',[10] which is not easy to square with his more anthropological use of the word. One can imagine a society without the arts and religion, or one in which life is not worth living, but not a way of life without a way of life.

The word 'nature', which is yet another of culture's opposites, contains a similar ambiguity. To say that rainwater is natural is to state a fact, whereas to claim that defrauding your customers is a natural part of being a banker is to formulate a value judgement. A former president of the US Federal Bank once remarked that he believed capitalism to be natural, in which case it may be that the citizens of ancient Persia were engaged in unnatural practices, along with the present-day tribes of the Amazon basin. There are postmodern theorists for whom the word 'natural' is thus to be avoided at all costs. For them, it is simply a devious way of 'naturalising' the cultural, so that things which are in fact changeable and contingent appear inevitable and unalterable. This assumes, oddly, that nature is immutable, which is scarcely the view of cosmetic surgeons or mining engineers. Yet the word 'nature' need have no such insidious implications. It is natural to mourn a dead friend. Childbirth is natural, and so is death. It is natural to be alarmed by a sudden wild shrieking in the night, or to dislike Russell Crowe. Nature has been hailed as a haven of serenity in which one can shelter from the turmoil of civilisation, but it can also be seen as just the opposite. On this view, it is civilisation which seeks to invest an unruly nature with a modicum of meaning. 'Nature is crazy', remarks Slavoj Žižek. 'Nature is chaotic and prone to wild, unpredictable and meaningless disasters, and we are exposed to its merciless whims. There is no such thing as Mother Earth . . . I don't think there is any natural order. Natural order is a catastrophe.'[11] It is not quite the kind of observation Wordsworth might have made to his friend Coleridge on a quiet stroll through the Lake District. For Žižek, the problem is not that nature is immutable but that it is all too volatile. As an idea, civilisation clips together the material and the spiritual. It tells us that there are a lot of sizeable buildings, ingenious facilities and elaborate organisations around, while also suggesting that all this tends to enhance our moral wellbeing. The notion of civilisation is, among other things, a judgement on people who are ill-starred enough not to have public libraries, central heating, Charlie Sheen or Cruise missiles. Instead, they inhabit something called a culture, which may mean that they have not yet evolved to the stage of wearing suits or skirts. Yet this is not always judged a defect. Oswald Spengler argues in *The Decline of the West* that all cultures eventually petrify and externalise themselves into civilisations, which suggests a decline from the organic to the mechanical. Until the advent of modern cultural technologies, civilisation was a more cosmopolitan phenomenon than culture, which has traditionally been a more parochial affair. There are some important exceptions to this rule: a Roman Catholic from Florida, for example, will have a huge amount in common with a Roman Catholic from Cambodia. Some cultural types (Freemasons, vegetarians, tuba players) can be found scattered across the planet. Generally speaking, however, culture has tended to reflect the life of a nation, region, social class or ethnic group. It is true that 'high' culture has long been a cosmopolitan affair, but popular culture did not go truly global until Charlie Chaplin happened along. John Stuart Mill writes of civilisation as involving:

> the multiplication of physical comforts; the advance and diffusion of knowledge; the decay of superstition; the facilities of mutual intercourse; the softening of manners; the decline of war and personal conflict; the progressive limitation of the tyranny of the strong over the weak; the great works accomplished throughout the world by the co-operation of multitudes . . . [12]

He then proceeds to list some of its negative aspects, not least the gross inequalities it generates between rich and poor. For Mill, then, civilisation would appear to cover the moral, material, social, political and intellectual, and as such to span both fact and value. It signifies a materially advanced, generally urban-based form of life, but at the same time suggests that one does things with style and sensitivity. It is civilised (in the descriptive sense) to wear trousers, but even more civilised (in the normative sense) to have your valet pull them on for you, or not to stroll into the drawing room with them bunched around your knees.

The ratio between these two aspects of civilisation can vary from place to place. The United States is sometimes accused of combining material prosperity with cultural crassness, whereas Britain, partly because it retains an aristocracy, has traditionally blended material affluence with polished social forms, cotton mills with county houses. The American novelist Henry James settled in England partly because he felt that he could write more readily in a country with royal palaces and ancient universities, dukedoms and debutantes. Fleeing from the 'invented', 'inorganic' nature of America, he discovered in English society a fine-spun fabric of 'manners, customs, usages, habits, forms'[13] which might lend his art a richer texture. Culture in the sense of art would be nourished by culture in the sense of an estimable way of life, not least because that way of life was already aesthetic in style and tone.

Elsewhere in his work, Mill writes:

we are accustomed to call a country civilised if we think it more improved; more eminent in the best characteristics of Man and Society; further advanced in the road to perfection; happier, nobler, wiser. This is one sense of the word civilisation. But in another sense it stands for that kind of improvement only, which distinguishes a wealthy and powerful nation from savages and barbarians.[14]

The distinction, once again, is between the normative and descriptive senses of the word. Perhaps there is an implication that all civilisation is perilously self-divided, since the former meaning of the term can always stand in judgement on the latter. Civilisation as moral progress is at odds with civilisation as beating orphans with a poker and sending small boys up chimneys. Ironically, the very forces which make for prosperity also help to refine our sensibilities, and thus make us more vigilant to the iniquities such prosperity brings in its wake. Industrial capitalist society produces the wealth to create such institutions as art galleries, universities and publishing houses, which can then take that same society to task for its greed and philistinism. In this sense, it is the role of culture to bite the hand that feeds it.

The word 'culture' was at first synonymous with 'civilisation', and continued for some time to be so; but it came eventually to signify a set of values that threw civilisation into question. Robert J.C. Young remarks on 'the startling fact that the notion of culture developed so that it was both synonymous with the mainstream of Western civilisation and antithetical to it. It was both civilisation and the critique of civilisation . . .'.[15] Culture, like civilisation, involves material institutions; but it can also be seen as a primarily spiritual phenomenon, and as such can pass judgement on social, political and economic activities. It is less under the sway of utility than civilisation, less hamstrung by pragmatic considerations. Simply by existing, culture in this sense of the term constitutes a critique of instrumental reason. Like 'civilisation', however, it can be a neutral term as well as a judgemental one. The phrase 'Nazi culture' might sound like an oxymoron, but it may simply mean the way of life of the Nazis, with no necessary overtone of approval. 'The Nazis detested culture', however, may well imply that what they abhorred was worth protecting from them. Sniffing glue may be cultural in the sense of part of your way of life, but not part of a commendable way of life. Culture in the sense of a body of artistic and intellectual work may be a descriptive term, with no high price tag attached to what it designates. Or it may be evaluative, but negatively so. There is, after all, a good deal of bad art and shoddy thinking. You can also be highly cultivated and morally bankrupt. The most masterly portrait of evil in modern literature, Thomas Mann's Adrian Leverkühn, is a magnificent composer.

It is true that a host of philosophers have assigned supreme value to culture in the sense of art. Not every great thinker has, however. Plato is hostile to art for political reasons, expelling the poets from his ideal republic. The greatest of modern philosophers, Immanuel Kant, purges art of its content and reduces it to pure form. For Hegel, modern art can no longer fulfil the vital role it performed in the ancient world, and must accordingly yield ground to philosophy. Jeremy Bentham, whose Utilitarian philosophy became the sovereign moral doctrine of nineteenth-century England, is a full-blooded philistine when it comes to aesthetic questions. The followers of Karl Marx hold that artistic culture is regularly pressed into the service of political hegemony, and so is to be treated with a certain scepticism. Nietzsche regards art as a necessary illusion. So does Arthur Schopenhauer, for whom it fulfils that most merciful of functions in a world of torment: escape. Thinkers from the Futurists to the Frankfurt School have rebuked art for offering us an imaginary resolution of real contradictions.

As for civilisation, there have been plenty of writers for whom it is more a matter of fact than a question of value – Thomas Hobbes, for example, or Jean-Jacques Rousseau, for whom it represents a lamentable decline from a more benign state of nature. The civilised in the sense of the mannered and urbane, of individual graces and stylish social forms, evokes Rousseau's petty-bourgeois disdain. Voltaire sees the history of civilisation as the story of how the rich grew bloated on the blood of the poor. Immanuel Kant thought that the source of civilised existence was social discord. Karl Marx considers that civilisation has only one progenitor, labour. It is a parent of which it is for the most part thoroughly ashamed, and which, like the Oedipal child, it often enough seeks to disavow. For Marx, labour is a form of intercourse with nature which gives birth to a social order; but because of the oppressive conditions under which such labour takes place, the order to which it gives rise is marked by conflict and violence.

In *Civilisation and its Discontents*, Sigmund Freud sees art as a sophisticated form of fantasy, and civilisation as a battle of lethally antagonistic forces. He is not at all convinced that the splendours of civilised existence are worth the price we pay for them in guilt, repression, sacrifice and self-loathing. Civilisation demands that we renounce our instinctual gratification, which in Freud's view plunges us into a state of 'permanent internal unhappiness'.[16] Leo Tolstoy writes scathingly of both art and civilised existence. Walter Benjamin famously regards civilisation as inseparably bound up with barbarism. It is a view anticipated by Jonathan Swift, who writes in his *A Tale of a Tub* (Section XIII) of 'how near [in humanity] the frontiers of height and depth border on each other'. There were many in the late nineteenth and early twentieth centuries for whom civilisation was only skin-deep. Beneath its surface lurked dark, malignant forces which threatened to irrupt into the daylight world at any moment. Scratch an English gentleman and you find a crazed beast. One might call it the *Lord of the Flies* syndrome.

It might be thought that civilisation is a functional affair, whereas culture is not. This, however, is too simple an antithesis. Civilisation contains a good many phenomena that have no particular point, such as Sarah Palin, breeding whippets or churning out 30 different brands of toothpaste. Culture, conversely, can fulfil a number of purposes. In many premodern societies, it serves a range of practical goals. In its moral and artistic sense, it can help us to live more abundantly. There is a difference, however, between activities which have an external goal and those whose ends are internal to them. The word 'praxis', which some left-wingers mistakenly employ as a synonym for 'practice', is better used to describe the latter type of activity. Art, sport and carousing in pubs with your friends all have a point, but it is not a point external to the activity itself, like knitting yourself a balaclava in order to rob a bank. Activities like this do not get you anywhere. They do not count as accomplishments. Not many people, when asked to list their skills on a job application, write 'getting drunk with friends'. There is even a theological dimension to this question. The doctrine of Creation is not about how the world began but the fact that it has no point. God made it just for fun, as part of his eternal self-delight. He might easily not have fashioned it at all, and from Sophocles to Schopenhauer there are those who have considered that this might well have been the more prudent option.

It is a remarkable fact that many of the most precious human activities are also the most aimless. Not all of them, to be sure: feeding the hungry and tending the sick are precious but not pointless. But kicking a ball about, having sex, playing with one's children, cultivating chrysanthemums and practising the clarinet have little utility value, if one leaves aside the Premier League footballers, opera stars, prostitutes, childminders, gardeners and musicians who practise such pursuits professionally. Such activities contain their goods, ends, grounds and reasons in themselves, and thus have an affinity with works of art. On this view, art is not what we live for, which would be a sterile kind of aestheticism; but it offers us a model of how to live, which is a more suggestive one. To aestheticise one's existence, as we shall see later in the case of Oscar Wilde, is not to strike elegant poses in the corner of drawing rooms or cover one's body with sequins but to dedicate oneself to pursuits of this kind. Aristotle thought that moral virtue was similarly self-grounding. It is what allows men and women to flourish, but it does not always result in such external goals as worldly success. Being virtuous may be conducive to a prosperous, contented existence, but it is no guarantee of it. A remarkable number of murder victims are described by their friends and family as having been sweet, bubbly, full of promise, blessed with hordes of friends and ready to do anything for others. People like this should walk warily at night. There are plenty of miserable moralists around, just as there are a number of cheerful blackmailers and flourishing fraudsters. Those who seek for justice may be slaughtered or imprisoned for their pains. Goodness in the form of innocence can render you a prey to others. In a predatory world, it is not always easy to distinguish virtue from gullibility. This is one reason why there is something quaint as well as imposing about the word 'virtue'.

Actions that have a point are generally performed for the sake of things that do not. A student who jots down an idea in her notebook does so because it might help her write a better essay. Writing a better essay may mean landing a higher class of degree, and landing a higher class of degree may result in securing a better paid job. Having more money means that she can spend her holidays in the Caribbean, visit the theatre, have dinner with her friends and generally live a richer, more rewarding life. But why should she want to do that? There is no very illuminating answer to that question. Explanations have to come to an end somewhere.

It is said that some years ago the authorities in New Orleans decided to give the names of figures from classical mythology to the city's streetcars, as they had to some of their streets. One of the cars was named Clio. Some local people called it 'C.L.10'. They expected signs on streetcars to be functional rather than decorative. The decorative, in the sense of whatever is surplus to simple need, is part of what we mean by culture. You need to give your child a name, but you do not have to call her Placenta. You need hair to protect your skull, but there is no necessity to dye it purple. It may be, however, that exceeding necessity is itself a necessity. The most searching investigation of this claim is *King Lear*. It belongs to our nature to transcend utility, delighting in things that have no practical point: jokes, for example, or green chartreuse. 'Superfluous' does not necessarily mean 'worthless'. On the contrary, what makes life worth living is not for the most part biologically indispensable to it. Food and drink are biologically essential, and are certainly for some people part of what makes life worth living, but pretty much any old food and drink will serve to keep you alive. Not throwing yourself out of a 10th storey window is essential for biological survival, but it is not what confers meaning on your life. It would be a grim prospect if the most precious aspect of one's existence was the thought that one had not hurled oneself to one's death from a great height. We should note, however, that while some necessities are common to all human cultures (food, sleep, shelter), others are not. There is a need for pedestrian crossings in Manhattan, but not in the Kalahari desert. What is essential for you may not be so for me. Most of us do not find private aircraft indispensable for our survival, but one suspects this may not be true of Madonna.

* * *

The word 'civilisation' refers to a world which is humanly manufactured. It involves rolling back nature to the point where we confront almost nothing in our surroundings that does not reflect ourselves. It is hard for us now to recapture the novelty of this kind of environment, compared to the largely nature-governed forms of life which preceded it. No doubt the need to break free of this collective narcissism is one reason why nature has staged a dramatic come-back in recent times. A world in which almost everything we encounter issues from our own hand would appear to be one bleached of transcendence. Instead, reality speaks simply of our own needs and powers. Perhaps this is one reason why a vital theme of Western civilisation has been desire, which can be seen as a secularised version of transcendence. It is no accident that the Faust legend bulks so large in the mythology of the West. Desire scoops out a hollow in humanity, overshadowing presence with absence and spurring us beyond the given to whatever eludes our grasp. In this sense, it can be seen as the very dynamic of civilised existence.

We can picture the various goods for which it strives, but desire itself runs deeper than representation. If it lies at the core of our being, it also signifies that within the self which is incorrigibly other to it. For psychoanalytic theory, desire is mostly what we are made of, but it has no particular regard for us, and certainly no tenderness for our welfare. On the contrary, it is as impersonal as moonlight. Since there are always more prizes to be attained, it signifies a kind of infinity, for which one historical name has been progress. Transcendence now lies not in the heavens but in the future. Yet since the future is in limitless supply, desire also entails perpetual dissatisfaction, turning our literary canons and political constitutions to ashes in our mouths. It signifies a flaw at the very heart of our fulfilment, an errancy of our being, a homelessness of the spirit. If Freud is to be credited, the only goal which will truly gratify it is death. It is for this reason that Rousseau looked on the endemic restiveness of civilisation with such distaste.

Culture, too, is humanly fashioned, even though the concept itself is derived from nature. It has an affinity with the word 'agriculture', as well with 'coulter', which means the blade of a plough. One of its earliest meanings is 'husbandry', or the tending of natural growth. Our term for some of the most exalted and urbane of human activities, then, has a humble rural root. From an allusion to everyday labour in the countryside, it comes to signify the finest fruits of the human spirit. Culture is a matter of grooming and nurturing. Like all labour, it reorders its raw materials. Yet the tending of natural growth holds together the idea of shaping with the notion of spontaneity. The growth in question is organic, not of our own making, but it needs to be regulated and refined. Culture involves agency, but also a certain receptiveness to the object, which will guide your hand in your effort to endow it with some significant form. It is therefore not clear how conscious or unconscious a phenomenon culture is, a question we shall return to later.

What needs to be refashioned is not only the world but the self, a process for which the key German term is *Bildung*. Human beings need to take themselves in hand, mould themselves into shape, make something rich and rare of their natural endowments. Culture is a matter of wholeness, but self-cultivation involves a form of self-division – of being artist and artefact in one body. On this theory, the self is ours on trust, as a set of capacities which it is our moral duty to develop to the full. It is as though we have been bequeathed some precious fledgling which it is our sacred duty to rear to maturity. The goal of human existence is self-realisation. The self is a project, a task in hand, a work in progress. Yet if it needs to be as intensively cultivated as a cabbage patch, doesn't this suggest that its natural condition leaves something to be desired? Perhaps there is an implication that the self in its common-or-garden state is alarmingly imperfect stuff, in which case there may be a troublingly dark subtext to the idea of culture. The raw materials we have to work with may be fatally flawed. Left to its own devices, nature will not redeem us. It harbours destructive forces as well as regenerative ones, and one of the problems of culture is how to defuse the former without diminishing the latter. Culture must preserve the vigour and freshness of the natural while curbing its disruptiveness. A paradigm of this is the work of art, which contains a vitality of content within a unity of form, thus fusing discipline with spontaneity. For Romantic theory, the exuberant energies of the artwork are always just on the point of spilling over their formal constraints, but in some miracle of tact or reticence are always just held back. Perhaps culture in the form-of-life sense should model itself on culture in the sense of art. Maybe the point of human existence is to turn oneself into a work of art. Oscar Wilde certainly thought so, as we shall see later.

That we *can* improve ourselves suggests that there are creative powers within the self; that we *need* to do so tells a less sanguine tale. Culture thus becomes a secular version of divine grace. Human nature is hospitable to it, as it is open to grace for the Christian, and is thus not entirely corrupt; yet it needs culture (or grace) in order to fulfil and transcend itself. And there are always those on whose natures nurture will never stick, as Prospero remarks of Caliban. That one's nature is inherently open to culture or grace does not entail that this bounteousness will be readily granted you. We shall see later that among these unregenerate types in the nineteenth century was the industrial working class.

CHAPTER TWO

Postmodern Prejudices

For some postmodern thinkers, the flourishing of a multiplicity of cultures is both a fact and a value. On this view, the existence of a diversity of life-forms, all the way from gay culture, catwalk culture and karaoke culture to Sikh culture, burlesque culture and Hell's Angels culture, is itself a cause for celebration. But this is surely mistaken. In fact, it is typical of the cant one finds on the subject these days. For one thing, diversity is perfectly compatible with hierarchy. For another thing, it is by no means certain that Hell's Angels culture is to be unambiguously applauded. In any case, diversity is not a value in itself. It is not self-evidently desirable that there should be fifty of something rather than one. It is plainly not true when it comes to neo-fascist parties. Nobody needs six thousand different brands of breakfast cereal. It may sound illogical to have only one monopolies commission, but more would be confusing. Having four hundred different aliases is probably not a good idea. You cannot have more than one biological mother or pair of ears. The fact that you can't is not a deficiency, however, let alone a tragedy. Having a rich diversity of spouses is likely to throw up the odd problem from time to time. Nor does much good flow from a prodigal array of autocrats. There are times when what is needed is not diversity but solidarity. It was not diversity that brought the apartheid system in South Africa to its knees, or plurality that toppled the neo-Stalinist regimes of Eastern Europe. Not all solidarity, to be sure, is to be affirmed. But postmodernism's lack of enthusiasm for the idea, along with its callow assumption that all forms of unity are 'essentialist', is a sure mark of its post-revolutionary character. Ethnically speaking, diversity is a positive value, but this should not lead us to overlook its role in consumerist ideology.

Postmodern apostles of plurality need to be more pluralistic about the notion. They should abandon the formalist dogma that it is always and everywhere to be extolled, whatever its actual content. If they were to do so, they might come to recognise in more pragmatic spirit that difference and diversity are sometimes beneficial and sometimes not. An American postmodernist wrote some years ago of the need to diversify social classes, as though having a new clutch of aristocracies in possession of even more thousands of acres of land would constitute an undoubted gain. Being more diverse about diversity, as well as acknowledging that difference may

31

differ from one context to another, would signal a genuine breakthrough for such thinkers. They might also try to be less absolutist about the idea of otherness, which most of them tend to affirm unreservedly. Some forms of otherness are to be esteemed, while others (a marauding gang of drug-dealers invading your council estate, for example) are not. There is nothing in the least irrational about being occasionally fearful of the other. It may be that one has yet to discover whether his or her intentions are amicable or hostile. Only sentimentalists imagine that strangers are always to be grappled to one's bosom. Some of these strangers are known as colonialists.

Most cultural theorists believe not only in a plurality of life-forms, but in a hybrid mixture of them. Hybridity may well be worth cultivating when it comes to ethnic matters, but it is not universally so. There is no harm in having political organisations made up of Jacobites, psychopaths, UFO buffs and Seventh Day Adventists. It is just that they will never achieve anything. As Marx points out, no mode of production in human history has been as hybrid, diverse, inclusive and heterogeneous as capitalism, eroding boundaries, collapsing polarities, merging fixed categories and pitching a diversity of life-forms promiscuously together. Nothing is more generously inclusive than the commodity, which in its disdain for distinctions of rank, class, race and gender will nestle up to anyone at all, provided they have the wherewithal to buy it. Capitalism is as much an enemy of hierarchy as cultural studies. Everyone is to be included, except those whose politics might undermine the very framework within which such inclusion occurs. There have been moves in Britain to hybridise the National Health Service by mixing private medical provision with public health care. One takes it that the champions of hybridity as a good in itself must endorse such a project.

The US Republican party is a hybrid organisation, including both liberal Republicans and Tea Party members, a fact that those for whom difference and diversity are unambiguous goods must surely welcome. Without those Republicans who believe that Barack Obama is a member of the Muslim Brotherhood and Al Qaeda a wing of the CIA, the party would be a far more drearily uniform set-up.

Not all uniformity is pernicious. Neither is all unity or consensus to be demonised as 'essentialist'. On the contrary, a great deal more of it would be thoroughly welcome. It is true that it takes all kinds to make a world, but it would help if all of these kinds clamoured for the abolition of child prostitution, or held that decapitating innocent civilians in the name of Allah is not the surest way to usher in utopia. It is unanimity we need on such questions, not variety. An English saying, no truer than many another, holds that it would be a funny world if we all thought alike. No doubt it would be a slightly more tedious world if everyone was opposed to capital punishment, but this would be a small price to pay for reducing the number of surplus corpses. Solidarity need not mean obliterating differences. Besides, some differences deserve to be obliterated – the material inequality between beggars and bankers, for example.

The fact that you believe in welcoming immigrants, whereas I believe in trying to sink their boats with a few well-aimed rounds of gunfire, is not an invigorating instance of human diversity. Different viewpoints are not to be valued simply because they are different viewpoints. If those who hold that cross-dressers should be fed to the crocodiles feel 'abused' (key postmodern term) when their view is robustly challenged, so be it. An opinion is not to be respected simply because somebody holds it. More or less any obnoxious viewpoint one can think up is probably held by somebody somewhere. There are right-wing Afrikaners who believe that Nelson Mandela was evil.

Groucho Marx famously remarked that he would be reluctant to join a club which included people like himself, and neither would one be keen to join a club run by war criminals. There is nothing in the least wrong in principle with exclusivity. Banning women from driving cars is deplorable, whereas shutting neo-Nazis out of the teaching profession is not. The discourse of cultural studies is itself strikingly exclusive: by and large, it deals in sexuality but not socialism, transgression but not revolution, difference but not justice, identity but not the culture of poverty. Politically correct students have taken to banning racists and homophobes from speaking on their campuses, but not quite so often exploiters of cheap labour or politicians who would like to see the back of trade unions. Such self-appointed censors tend to sing the praises of marginality without recognising that some of those who are currently marginal should at all costs remain so. Serial killers and psychopathic cult leaders rank prominently among them. There are forms of life that are not only worthless but which should be energetically rooted out: paedophile rings, for example, or men who sell women into sexual slavery. Neither are all minorities to be enthusiastically embraced. The ruling class is one such minority, as are people who enjoy slicing bits off other people and cooking them for supper. An uncritical affirmation of margins and minorities usually goes hand-in-hand with a suspicion of consensuses and majorities. This is because postmodernism is too young to remember a time when mass political movements rocked the state far more vigorously than any margin or minority has proved capable of doing. It tends to be unaware of how deeply its political views are shaped by its own political history, or rather by the lack of it.

A concern with pluralism, difference, diversity and marginality has yielded some precious gains. But it has also served to displace attention from various more material issues. In fact, in some quarters culture has become a way of not talking about capitalism. Capitalist society relegates whole swathes of its citizenry to the scrap heap, but is exquisitely sensitive about not offending their beliefs. Culturally speaking, we are all to be granted equal respect, while economically speaking the gap between the clients of food banks and the clients of merchant banks looms ever larger. The cult of inclusivity helps to mask these material differences. The right to dress, worship or make love as one wishes is revered, while the right to a decent wage is denied. Culture acknowledges no hierarchies, but the educational system is ridden with them. Speaking with a Yorkshire accent is no obstacle to becoming a television newscaster, but being a Trotskyist is. It is against the law to insult ethnic minorities in public, but not to insult the poor. Any adult is free to sleep with any other who is not related by blood, but they are not also free to undermine the state. Sexual experimenters are treated with indulgence by metropolitan liberals, while strikers are met with suspicion. Difference is to be welcomed, but full-blooded conflict is not. Nobody should arrogate the right to tell others what to do, an attitude which tax evaders find mightily convenient.

It is disingenuous to praise cultural diversity without reckoning its appalling cost. If the globe were populated only by gay Malaysians, with the odd straight Malaysian thrown in to keep the show on the road, it would doubtless be a more monochrome place. But it would almost certainly be a less bloody one as well. It is true that gay Malaysians might split into rival factions as quickly as the sectarian schoolboys of *Lord of the Flies*. Uniformity is no guarantee of a quiet life. But the conflicts that ensued would probably be nothing compared to the noise of hacking and gouging which has been the soundtrack of human history to date, and for which ethnic, national and cultural antagonisms have been in some measure responsible. Gerard Manley Hopkins celebrates what he calls the pied and dappled nature of things, but fails to touch on its darker subtext.

'The drunkenness of things being various', in Louis MacNeice's phrase, is by no means to be sniffed at. But neither is it to be absolutised. One problem with the concepts of difference and hybridity is that they tend to diffuse conflict. And conflict may be essential if differences of an objectionable kind are to be overcome. Puce and vermilion are different but not mutually contentious. You and I cannot clash over the question of whether rock has had its day if you have in mind a style of music and I am thinking of a type of candy. Cultural theory is in danger of taking the pain out of hybridity and plurality. It attends to its angelic features but not to its demonic ones. The modernist artists who spurned their native soil for a more cosmopolitan style of existence, mingling with colleagues from other lands in some polyglot cafe, found this an enthralling emancipation. But it could also mean that they were rootless, homesick and unhappy. A modest degree of identity and stability are essential to any human life. Permanent disorientation is not a politics, whatever Gilles Deleuze might imagine.

* * *

In response to a social order in which culture seems veritably wall-to-wall, some postmodern theorists from the 1980s onwards came to embrace the doctrine of culturalism, for which culture in human affairs goes all the way down.[1] All talk of nature became darkly suspect, at just the point, ironically, when environmentalism was breaking upon the world. Whenever the word 'nature' occurs in a postmodern text, it is usually to be found coyly draped in scare quotes. Human beings were no longer to be seen as natural, material animals, with needs and capabilities common to them as a species; instead, they were cultural creatures all the way through. To point to the vital features that they share by virtue of their common humanity was to suppress cultural difference in the name of a spurious universalism. Economic and political issues were reframed as cultural ones. Natures and essences had to go, since they were mistakenly thought to freeze things into unalterable forms. The doctrine of anti-essentialism was hailed as inherently radical, despite the fact that it can be found in the work of a number of ardently anti-leftist thinkers.

Change was assumed to be positive in itself, as though bartering your children for a clapped-out Ford was a cause for congratulation. In the climate of advanced capitalism, everything was to be plastic, provisional, mutable, malleable, disposable; and culture, astonishingly, was thought to be far more pliable than nature. The sheer intractability of culture – the fact that it is a lot easier to move mountains than it is to eradicate sexism – was conveniently overlooked. The obtuse tenacity of certain cultural habits was set to one side. In this climate, whatever was purely given, as the body is given, seemed something of a scandal. Human flesh was now stuff to be disciplined, pummelled, bedecked, inscribed and remoulded. Regions of the globe which offered some resistance to Western hegemony were also to be cuffed into shapes more gratifying to the Masters of the Universe.

The prejudice that everything in the world is cultural, including bleeding, Mont Blanc and dying of liver failure, is generally to be found coupled with cultural relativism. Such relativism denies that there are any universal truths or values. Instead, all such claims, including moral ones, are relative to a specific form of life. Whether this claim itself is culturally relative is not an easy question to answer. The general idea is that rather than condemning the headhunters, we should seek to understand them, setting such practices in their cultural contexts. But to set an event in its context may be to sharpen one's disapproval, not alleviate it. Besides, if actions are acceptable once viewed in cultural context, then this must apply to our own behaviour as well. Colonising other nations, waging global warfare and poisoning the planet is just what we Westerners tend to do. There is an age-old cultural tradition among us known as invading other people's countries, which some radicals appear to find objectionable; but since a number of such leftists also regard the concept of objective truth as an oppressive power ploy, there is no pressing need for them to take their protests against this practice too seriously. In a similar way, we surely cannot be so epistemologically naive as to imagine that the claim that men and women were once transported in chains from Africa to America corresponds to the 'facts'. It is also worth noting that those who feel horrified by the slave trade tend to assume that its victims are likely to feel much the same; but why should they smugly universalise their own convictions in this manner, arrogantly projecting them on to individuals with very different scales of value? Can we really rule out the possibility that the members of other cultures might actually enjoy being kidnapped and worked to death? Are we not suppressing differences and assuming a universal human nature in too quickly dismissing this hypothesis?

It may appear to some of our erstwhile colonial subjects that we have visited various atrocities upon them from time to time, but a particularly bold-faced cultural relativist might argue that this is the case only from their own standpoint. It is an opinion conditioned by their culture, of no more import than any other such viewpoint, and we erstwhile colonial conquerors are thus perfectly free to repudiate it. It is simply their story. There is certainly no neutral ground on which we might adjudicate between their sombre narrative and our own tales of imperial glory, since neutrality, disinterestedness and objectivity are deemed to be ideological illusions. Other nations can therefore no more reprove us than we can censure them. Besides, telling other cultures what they should or shouldn't do is a prime example of ethnic supremacism. Truth is just what some group or individual holds to be true – what makes sense from their local perspective. Some people maintain that slavery was a crime against humanity, while others insist that the slaves had nobody to blame but themselves, but by what divine right are we to judge between these opinions? Would we not need to resort to some illusory vantage-point of absolute truth in order to do so? Surely the only way to be sure that torturing toddlers is undesirable is to adopt an omniscient standpoint! The Russian Margarita Simonyan, who runs one of the Kremlin's TV channels, has argued that there is no such thing as truth, merely a diversity of narratives and interpretations. That Vladimir Putin is in the habit of having his political opponents murdered may make for an absorbing narrative, but one should not be so epistemologically naive as to mistake it for the truth. Dissent in such places may be violently suppressed, but surely not 'objectively' so.

Cultural relativism is a vastly implausible position. Only racists believe that it is all right to rape and murder in Borneo but not in Brighton. There is nothing 'elitist' or 'hierarchical' in holding that some standpoints are better or truer than others. As the philosopher Richard Rorty once remarked, there is no need to engage in debate with people who hold that any view of a particular question is as good as any other, since there aren't any. It is true that those who advocate

41

cultural relativism generally do so for the most admirable of reasons. They are reluctant to absolutise their own values, open as they are to the life-forms of others. But what if such tolerance is no part of my own way of life? Should you be open to this too? Who are you to reject my conviction that tolerance is a mistake?

For most culturalists, the belief that there are universal foundations to human existence is an illusion. Cultures are free-standing. They are not to be seen as resting on anything more fundamental than themselves, such as God, *Geist*, matter, human nature, the life-force, the dialectic, the march of history or the structure of the cosmos. Even if such weighty infrastructures do indeed lie at their root, each culture (so the argument goes) would conceive of them in its own idiosyncratic way, so that they would cease to be truly universal. What this means, however, is that culture becomes the new foundation. To see everything as relative to culture is to turn culture itself into an absolute. It is now culture that one cannot dig beneath, as it used to be God or nature or the self. One could dig beneath culture only by cultural means (concepts, techniques, methods of inquiry and so on), which means that one would not be digging beneath it at all.

There is, however, something more deep-seated than culture, namely the material conditions which make it both possible and necessary. It is because human beings are material animals of a peculiar kind that they give birth to cultures in the first place, and it is also because of this material nature that they need to do so. All men and women are born prematurely, emerging from the womb unable to survive by themselves; and unless culture in the sense of systems of nurture moves in on them right away, they will quickly die. Culture in this broad sense of the term is crucial to our survival, in contrast to cultureless creatures like foals and baby giraffes who are born, stagger to their feet, lick themselves down and trot calmly off into the middle distance. Culture is not identical with our nature, as the culturalists claim; rather, it is *of* our nature. It belongs to what Marx calls our 'species being'. By virtue of our species being, we are capable of complex forms of labour and communication, which lay the groundwork for what we know as culture or civilisation. We also need such labour and communication if we are to survive. Badgers and squirrels relate to their environments in a direct bodily way; humans, by contrast, have the sort of bodies that allow them to extend themselves across the globe. If this is a source of achievement, it can also be a cause of catastrophe.

There is another sense in which culture is not the baseline of humanity. To construct a culture in the sense of tennis clubs, herb gardens, haute cuisine, hairstyles, radio stations and so on, you need to generate an economic surplus. There can be no flourishing of culture in this sense of the word in societies in the grip of material scarcity, though there will certainly be culture in the sense of language, kinship, ceremonies, conventions, organised ways of doing things and the like. People who need to invest most of their energy in the business of staying alive have neither the time nor resources to throw sherry parties or dash off epic poems. A professional caste of artists and intellectuals, as Marx recognises, becomes possible only when not everyone needs to labour for most of the time. Only then can one establish a full-scale division of labour, as a number of privileged individuals are released from the necessity to toil to become bards, shamans, chieftains, philosophers, supervisors, archbishops, disc jockeys, duchesses and so on. Culture, then, has its material conditions. In this sense, it is not the last word. It is the fruit not only of labour but of exploitation and unhappiness. 'How much blood and cruelty lie at the root of all "good things"!', exclaims Nietzsche,[2] who thought such suffering perfectly acceptable if it produced both the Parthenon and geniuses like himself.

* * *

Ludwig Wittgenstein argues in his *Philosophical Investigations* that what is simply 'given' is what he calls forms of life, or what we might call cultures. Forms of life are given in the sense that there is no rational justification for them. There is no logical reason why one should use hieroglyphs rather than an alphabet, or greet someone by rubbing noses rather than shaking hands. Such things are their own foundation. When an argument touches on them, Wittgenstein observes, it is as though one's spade hits rock bottom and one has simply to stop digging. Not everything stands in need of explanation, and not every explanation needs to be backed up with a more fundamental one. In this sense, certain ways of doing things are beyond question, and certain judgements on them are ruled out of court. There is a point to being a VIP because you do not have to queue to board an aircraft, but there is no point to being Japanese. It is not superior to being Iranian, any more than one could claim that the grammar of Pali has a splendour unknown to the grammar of Portuguese. Being Japanese is not an achievement. The Japanese win prizes, but they do not win prizes for being Japanese. This is one sense in which forms of life are simply given.

If we are asked why we celebrate birthdays or measure distances in miles, the answer, Wittgenstein would suggest, is simply that 'this is what we do'. This is not to deny that some ways of doing things may be more advantageous than others. We do not measure distances in python-lengths because it would be fatiguingly complicated. We would need an inconvenient number of digits to record the distance between the Earth and Jupiter. When it comes to miles versus kilometres, however, or green motorway signs versus blue ones, there isn't much to choose between them. Such customs are not rational, which is not to claim that they are irrational either. They could not be said to be right or wrong, any more than it is wrong to put the verb at the end of the sentence in German.

In this sense, Wittgenstein's argument would seem to chime with certain postmodern prejudices. But this is not the case. He was perfectly prepared to make rigorous judgements on cultural habits. For one thing, the fact that a practice is simply given, with no very persuasive rationale, does not mean that one should endorse it. The custom of wearing a tie to High Table in Wittgenstein's Cambridge college was of this kind, but he himself thought it ridiculous and refused to kowtow to it. There may be reasons for wishing an event to be formal, but there is no reason why wearing a tie around your neck, rather than a piece of old rope around your ankle, should count as this. You can have reasons to reject something that exists without a reason. For another thing, the fact that there are conventions and procedures which lie beyond either criticism or justification does not entail that all of our practices do so, any more than the fact that a grammar lies beyond criticism or justification entails that whatever propositions it gives rise to are similarly beyond dispute. Those who relish differences should note the distinction between cultural habits we would find it almost impossible to shake off, such as imagining the future as lying in front of us, and practices such as female genital mutilation or the manufacture of chemical weapons, which present us with no such difficulty. Wittgenstein himself was no fan of the modern world, and was not slow to voice his patrician disdain for it. In fact, he pulled off the remarkable feat of rejecting middle-class modernity from both the political left and the political right.

Armed robbers who are apprehended by the police do not tend to say 'This is just what I do.' It is true that if you are reared in a culture which does not count beyond seven, you have no choice but to conform to this custom, but there is no human culture in which strangling other people simply because you happen to feel like it is an acceptable practice. You cannot justify using women as sex slaves on the grounds that it is a vital component of your culture. This would amount to claiming that what you do is acceptable because you habitually do it, which is hardly the most cogent line of defence. The fact that one cannot pick a quarrel with the grammar of one's language does not mean that one cannot protest against the use of that grammar for the purpose of racial abuse.

Even so, to be critical of a culture involves taking a number of its features for granted. You can censure the prime minister for blatant favouritism only if you assume that eminent people can be as corrupt as ordinary ones. One could imagine a form of life which would find such an assumption unintelligible. Generally speaking, Wittgenstein's point is that not everything can be up for grabs at any given moment. To be able to criticise, you must do so within certain categories that (at least for the present) you accept as given, just as a doubt is possible only against a background of taken-for-granted certainties. You cannot doubt whether the car keys are still on the hall table unless you assume that there are such things as physical objects, that they are capable of being shifted from one location to another, that they do not spontaneously transport themselves and so on. A doubt which had no such context, like Descartes's claim to doubt everything, would simply have no force. It would be like a cog in the machine of language which failed to mesh with anything around it. Nobody can be a sceptic about everything. But this does not mean that they are doomed to be the dupes of everything either.

CHAPTER THREE

The Social Unconscious

WE HAVE SEEN that for Wittgenstein there is a good deal in any form of life that must be taken for granted. This is not a matter of complacency. In order to protest against racist assaults, for example, you must take it for granted that skin colour is not a badge of inferiority. Convictions of this kind can of course be explicitly formulated, and sometimes need to be; but many of our beliefs exist in a semi-inchoate form that one might call the social unconscious – that vast repository of instincts, prejudices, pieties, sentiments, half-formed opinions and spontaneous assumptions which underpins our everyday activity, and which we rarely call into question. In fact, some of these assumptions run so deep that we probably could not query them without some momentous change in our way of life, one which might make them fully perceptible for the first time. They include the belief that global nuclear warfare would not be particularly agreeable, though not the 'belief' that human beings die, since we would not call a belief something which we could not possibly imagine disbelieving. It is possible to believe that National Rail is run by the Knights Templar, but not to believe that you have two hands.

This social unconscious is one thing we mean by culture. That this should be so is ironic, since culture in the sense of the arts and intellectual work ranks among the most finely conscious of human activities. So culture would seem to be both more intensely self-aware than most of what we do, and a good deal less so. In the latter sense of the word, it constitutes the invisible colour of everyday life, the taken-for-granted texture of our workaday existence, too close to the eyeball to be fully objectified. It is this which Jacques Lacan calls 'the Other', meaning the untotalisable context within which all our speech and behaviour acquire their sense. It is a context that so constitutes us that for the most part we are oblivious to its operations. In fact, if we were continually trying to investigate its workings we might not be able to function at all, rather as we would be tongue-tied were we to be conscious at the moment of utterance of the grammatical structures that allow us to speak in the first place. In a similar way, Freud sees the ego as necessarily blind to much that goes into its making. What puts it in place must necessarily be absent from it. It emerges only through a painful repression of the processes which constitute it, a trauma from which it will never fully recover. Nobody manages entirely to live down the primordial catastrophe known as infancy. One reason for this failure is that human beings are sexual animals, and sexuality is where we are most infantile, not where we are most mature.

Perversely, then, a degree of repression is actually good for you. Self-blindness and a certain saving amnesia are what allow us to flourish, for Friedrich Nietzsche as well as for Sigmund Freud. Too much repression, to be sure, is likely to make us ill. We can fall sick of unrequited desire, which is what Freud knows as neurosis, and by which we are all afflicted to some extent. For Freud, the human animal is the sick animal, even if we are sick in ways that are productive as well as debilitating. We can, to be sure, engage in self-reflection. Thinking critically about their situation is part of the way human beings, as opposed to tortoises, are bound up with the world. It does not mean standing at some illusory Archimedean point outside it, a claim advanced by a number of thinkers (Richard Rorty and Stanley Fish among them) who wish to discredit the idea of a radical critique. In Freud's view, however, such self-reflection is not enough to save us. Nobody was ever cured of their neurosis simply by being smart about their own psyche. Indeed, this is more likely to be part of the problem that the solution. There is a blind spot at the core of the subject which is constitutive of it, but which could never be dredged to consciousness by simple self-reflection. It would be like trying to pick oneself up by one's bootstraps, or trying to see oneself seeing something. This is why psychoanalytic therapy is in the end a matter of doing rather than saying. The scene of analysis is a theatre, a project, a stretch of hard labour, a mutual transaction or dramatic performance, not in the first place a question of theory.

For Marx, this self-blindness is also true of class-society. All the most vital social processes, he comments in *Capital*, go on 'behind the backs' of the agents engaged in them. One might call this the political unconscious, whereby the meaning of one's action for oneself is not identical with its meaning for the Other, in the sense of the field of language or social system as a whole. You might consider yourself a conscientious lord of the manor, sensitive to the needs of your serfs, but this is mostly a way of rationalising your privileged status. The truth of one's actions, so to speak, is located in the Other, in the whole region of signification, not in one's intentions or experience. It is as though the action occurs in one place and its meaning in another. If the true significance of what we do were apparent to us, we might see the need to change our behaviour. What prevents this from happening, in Marx's view, is ideology. It is through the medium of ideology that we provide ourselves with interpretations of our behaviour which serve to deflect or disguise its true significance; so that what we do, and what we say we do, are structurally at odds with each another.

Ideology is not the same as culture. We have seen that culture, in one sense of the term, is a matter of values and symbolic practices, whereas ideology denotes those values and symbolic practices which at any given time are caught up in the business of maintaining political power. Culture, then, is the more capacious concept, and much of what it contains may be ideologically innocent, at least for most of the time. There is no very interesting sense in which collecting late Victorian paperweights can be seen as sustaining a sovereign power. Not everything in a culture is ideological, though anything in it might become so. Culture is a functionally variable term, in the sense that what may be cultural in one context may not be so in another. This is particularly true if one thinks of culture as what makes life worth living rather than what keeps it going. Exchanging gifts may be a cultural practice for us moderns, but in some premodern social orders it may be bound up with economic necessity. Drinking alcohol is a cultural affair, but it would cease to be so if it was the only way of quenching an intolerable thirst. Survivors of an air crash in some remote terrain who break open the drinks locker are not having a party. An activity may be both cultural in the sense of decorative or non-functional, and non-cultural in the sense of fulfilling some biological need. You may wear a head-dress in Qatar as a badge of your cultural identity, but also to avoid getting sunstroke.

Ideology, too, is functionally variable. What may be ideological at one time or place may not be so at another. A casual flexing of the arm muscles in one context may signify a fascist salute in another. That there are both white and red roses is ideological only if these flowers become insignia in a power struggle. TV weather forecasts become ideological only if the presenter obsessively insists on how much more dreary the weather is in North Korea than in the United States. It is not ideological for infant schools to teach their pupils how to fasten their shoelaces, but it is ideological to teach them that their talents must be judiciously invested in order to ensure the most profitable return. 'I do like a nice strong cup of tea' is not in itself ideological, but it could become so, if, for example, it was pre-arranged code for 'the troops are to open fire immediately on the student protesters'.

One cannot speak of cultural practices in terms of intelligence. It is not clever to drink Bacardi, or boneheaded to be a flamenco dancer. Ideology, however, is another matter. Though a good deal of it can be plausible, intricate and theoretically elaborate, its presence often makes itself felt in a sudden unaccountable drop in the intellectual temperature. It is when otherwise shrewd, worldly-wise men and women come up with such propositions as 'The unemployed could always find work if they tried', or 'Muslims will outnumber non-Muslims in Britain by 2025' that one can detect the working of forces which outflank the rational.

Culture is not always a medium of power. It can also be a mode of resistance to it. We shall see in a moment that this is true of the political domain for the philosopher Edmund Burke, but it can be true of artistic and intellectual culture as well. The claim that the literary canon is a bastion of political benightedness, for example, is plainly absurd. The truth is that a good deal of 'high' or minority literature is far more politically subversive than most popular culture. In English terms alone, one has only to think of Milton, Blake, Shelley, Byron, Hazlitt, Paine, Wollstonecraft, Dickens, Ruskin, Morris, Woolf and Orwell, not to speak of a host of others. It is hard to argue that *Friends* or *Sex and the City* outdo these authors in revolutionary zeal, or that Lady Gaga and Robbie Williams offer us utopian visions of human comradeship to rival Blake's prophetic works. It is true that the music of Justin Bieber reaches a great many ordinary people, but so does chicken pox. Shakespeare spoke up for communism, Milton championed regicide, Blake and Shelley were political revolutionaries, Flaubert and Baudelaire detested the middle classes, Rimbaud was an anarchist and Tolstoy denounced private property. Virginia Woolf's *A Room of One's Own* is one of the most radical non-fictional texts ever produced by a British literary author. It is true that the idea of a literary canon has been used often enough in objectionably elitist ways, but much of what that canon contains runs counter to such politics. Even so, we should recall that the distinction between 'high' and 'popular' culture does not correspond to one between good and bad. Much popular culture is of superb quality, while the literary canon contains a fair amount of inferior stuff – whole stretches of Wordsworth's poetry, for example. If a handful of a writer's works make it into the canon, a good deal of his or her less distinguished writing will tend to follow suit, with the result that the canon is quite often hard to defend even by its own criteria of judgement.

* * *

No thinker has articulated the idea of culture as the social unconscious more magnificently than the eighteenth-century writer and politician Edmund Burke. Despite this, one suspects that Burke's name is rarely if ever mentioned on cultural studies courses. Perhaps this is because he is associated with a conservative reverence for monarchy, church and nobility – a set of allegiances which spurred him to become Britain's most ferocious, implacable opponent of the French Revolution. Yet Burke was not a Tory but a liberal Whig, who believed strongly in the need for reform. He was, for example, among the foremost opponents of slavery of his age. Though he denounced the French Revolution, he was by no means opposed to revolution as such. He was an enthusiast of the Norman Conquest of Britain, which brought his own family to his native land, as well as of the so-called Glorious Revolution of 1688. When America grew disaffected with British rule, Burke came to believe that reform in the colony was out of the question; that violent revolution there, however regrettable, was inevitable; and that it was his own nation which was driving its colonial subjects headlong into insurgency. As a Member of Parliament, he sought to dissuade his fellow politicians from using force against their American colonial subjects. Once they rose in revolt, he championed their struggle against British rule.

Strictly speaking, however, Britain was not Burke's own nation, which accounts in part for his ferocious critique of its colonial policies. He hailed from England's oldest colony, Ireland, and his oratory, according to one contemptuous English politician, John Wilkes, 'stank of whisky and potatoes'. Though of an ancient Irish family, he spent some time as a child in an open-air school in County Cork, spoke the Irish language and developed a deep compassion for the Irish rural poor. Despite being one of Westminster's most illustrious politicians, Burke had strong sympathies with underground peasant militants in his homeland, and was outraged by the reprisals visited upon them by the British government. When he writes of the Defenders, one of the leading groups of Irish insurgents, that 'Catholic Defenderism is the only restraint on Protestant Ascendancy',[1] he allies himself unequivocally with violent rebellion in Ireland – and this on the part of a man who has been venerated over the centuries as a fount of right-wing wisdom. If he failed to lend unambiguous support to the revolutionary United Irishmen, he nevertheless verged on complicity with them. Burke had no love of political revolution, but he was convinced that it was almost always provoked by the unjust dealings of a sovereign power, and that after a while it became unavoidable. 'Let the mind of man be ever so inured to servitude,' he remarks, 'still there is a point where oppression will arouse it to injustice.'[2] When such a point is reached, the rulers in Burke's view have no one to blame but themselves.

Burke was virulently hostile to Ireland's Anglo-Irish governing elite, and railed against their indifference to the plight of the Irish poor. Their aim, he writes with a typical touch of hyperbole, is 'to keep a dominion over the rest [of the people] by reducing them to absolute slavery under a military power'.[3] The rights of landlords, he insisted, were not absolute, but must serve to promote the common good. Though a Protestant himself, he was the staunchest, most highly placed apologist for the Irish Catholic cause in the eighteenth century, and decried the so-called Penal Laws which served to keep the Catholic population in its place. The Laws, he claims, were 'as well fitted for the oppression, impoverishment, and degradation of a people, and the debasement in them, of human nature itself, as ever proceeded from the perverted ingenuity of man'.[4] In fact, the Penal Laws were nothing like as monstrous as this piece of rhetoric suggests (Burke has a talent for lurid exaggeration), but their symbolic value as a sign of Protestant supremacy was nonetheless profound. It was largely through Burke's influence that they were finally dismantled.

Power, Burke believed, was legitimate only if it was founded on 'a community of interests, and a sympathy in feelings and desires between those who act in the name of any description of people, and the people in whose name they act'.[5] It was just this community of interests and sentiments that he found disastrously lacking in Ireland, as well as in the colonial relationship between Britain and America. 'Power', he suggests, 'gradually extirpates from the mind every humane and gentle virtue. Pity, benevolence, friendship are things almost unknown in high places.'[6] 'Power and authority', he writes of America, 'are sometimes bought by kindness; but they can never be begged as alms by an impoverished and defeated violence.'[7] The American insurrectionists, he considered, were a genuine case of a people demanding and deserving their freedom. 'There is no reason', he comments, 'why one people should voluntarily yield any degree of pre-eminence to another, but on a supposition of great affection and benevolence toward them.'[8] Burke believed in empire, to be sure, but an empire bound together by culture rather than coercion.

Consensus, Burke insists, should be true of any political set-up:

Men are not tied to one another by paper and seals. They are led to associate by resemblances, by conformities, by sympathies. Nothing is so strong a tie of amity between nation and nation as correspondence in laws, customs, manners, and habits of life. They have more than the force of treaties in themselves. They are obligations written in the heart.[9]

These bonds, he remarks, though as light as air, are as strong as links of iron. 'The only firm seat of authority', he declares, 'is in the minds, affections and interests of the people.'[10] (These, it should be noted, are the sentiments of a Whig free-marketer and disciple of Adam Smith who objected to almost any intervention in the market. Not all of Burke's political attitudes are to be commended.) The state in his view is a partnership between those who are living, those who are dead and those who are yet to be born. As such, it is not 'to be considered as nothing better than a partnership agreement in a trade of pepper and coffee, calico or tobacco, or some other such low concern'.[11] Instead, it should be anchored in customs, traditions and manners. What matters in securing one's power, as Antonio Gramsci was to insist over a century later, is the rich tapestry of habits and heritages we know as civil society, and if Burke felt its allure, it is partly because, like Henry James after him, he hailed from a nation which was deficient in such institutions.

Grounding one's power in custom and sentiment was palpably not the case with Britain's rule in Ireland, but it was just as lacking in its sovereignty over India. What Burke sees when he contemplates the jewel in the imperial crown is 'an utterly ruined, undone, depopulated country, [one] saved from literal and exceptionless depopulation only by the exhibition of scattered bands of wild, naked, meagre, half-famished wretches who [rend] heaven with their cries and howling'.[12] Spurning the myth of Oriental barbarism, he insists of the Indians that 'their morality is equal to ours . . . and I challenge the world to show, in any modern European book, more true morality and wisdom than is to be found in the writings of Asiatic men in high trust, and who have been counsellors to princes'.[13] The people of the country, he declares, were 'for ages civilised and cultivated; cultivated by all the arts of polished life, while we were yet in the woods'.[14] As one commentator observes:

> Burke was one of the first major European thinkers, and one of the first writers in the traditional canon of Western political theory, to have made a serious effort to understand a non-Western civilisation and to incorporate his findings into his general political thought . . . In taking India seriously, Burke was at the same time one of the first major Western thinkers to grapple with the moral and political problems of European empire over non-Western nations.[15]

One might add that he also ranked among the first Western thinkers to take seriously the question of group or collective rights, in contrast to a promotion of individual rights which could be perfectly compatible with national or racial supremacy.

Political power, in Burke's view, can flourish only through a sensitivity to culture. It involves 'studying the genius, the temper, the manners of the people, and adapting to them the laws that we establish'.[16] If nations are to be governed at all, then it must be 'upon their own principles and maxims and not upon ours'.[17] It is the rulers who must conform to the people, not vice versa, but the cultural differences between Britain and India yawn too wide for this to be feasible. The same is true in Burke's opinion of the disabling geographical gulf between Britain and America. India in particular is cut off from the West 'by manners, by principles of religion, and [by] inveterate habits as strong as nature itself',[18] and its rich diversity of life-forms is impossible to assimilate to a single, externally imposed authority. These circumstances, Burke argues, cast serious doubt on the very idea of attempting to govern the place. He was a passionate opponent of the East India Company, a powerful arm of British authority in India, and sought to impeach its head, Warren Hastings, before the Westminster parliament.

'Our conquest [of India],' Burke complains, 'after twenty years, is as crude as it was on the first day.'[19] The colonialists, he protests, have no more habits in common with the indigenous people than if they still resided in England; and if they were to abandon the country tomorrow, they would leave no vestige of benevolent government behind them. In fact, he venomously adds, they would leave no sign of possession superior to that of a tiger or orang-utan. Throughout the 'inglorious period of [its] dominion', England, Burke writes, 'has erected no churches, no hospitals, no palaces, no schools; England has built no bridges, made no high roads, cut no navigations, dug out no reservoirs'. Every previous conqueror has left some monument behind him, but not the British. Instead, in India as elsewhere, the imperial forces have drawn 'from the wretchedness and misery of persons destitute and undone . . . the great sources of our wealth, our strength, and our power'.[20]

Burke did not see barbarism simply as a condition that civilisation had left behind. On the contrary, he was aware of how it can be the product of civilisation itself. Barbarism and civilisation might be sequential, but they were also synchronic. Whole cultures had been violated by the march of civilised society. Commerce, Burke felt, far from improving such social orders, might drive them to their ruin. Given his experience of Ireland, he was keenly aware of the wretchedness involved in the civilising process, though he had few illusions about a mythical golden age. In *A Vindication of Natural Society*, he sees the true scandal of civilisation as lying not in the fact that its origins are bathed in blood, but that this violence persists as a permanent feature of it. Civilisation may be an achievement to be applauded, but it exacts a fearful cost in human suffering. What Burke saw in the excesses of the French Revolution was a form of civilised savagery, but he perceived much the same ferocity in his own adopted nation. Britain, he charges, has become 'a land of blood' as a result of its disreputable conduct in India.

That native Americans were a naturally bloodthirsty bunch was a conviction that Burke shared with his English colleagues. Unlike most of his fellow parliamentarians, however, he held that the final responsibility for the crimes of subjugated peoples lay with their colonial masters. Native Americans might be naturally wild, but their brutishness had been intensified, not alleviated, by white rule. Violence, Burke considered, was often enough the monstrous offspring of injustice. What drove the downtrodden to commit atrocities was the insolence of authority. This is not to say that he excused the outrages perpetrated by colonial peoples. On the contrary, he had no hesitation in censuring them. He was not some dewy-eyed sentimentalist for whom the conquerors could do no right and the vanquished no wrong. Nor was he a cultural relativist. On the contrary, he was aware of how conveniently such relativism could let his own nation off the hook. For the British in India to appeal to the country's alien conditions to justify their crimes was in his eyes a piece of shabby sophistry. It is part of Burke's polemic against Warren Hastings that ethical imperatives are universal rather than parochial; that moral values do not bend to shifts of geographical locale; and that the same standards of liberty and justice must prevail among the Indian people as among the British. Burke had a passion for the concrete and contextual, and a suspicion of the abstract and universal. Yet he was not opposed to universal principles, simply to the assumption that they can be mechanically applied without due attention to circumstance.

* * *

From beginning to end, then, Burke's theme is plain: culture is more fundamental than law or politics. 'Nations', he writes, 'are not primarily ruled by laws; less by violence'.[21] It is 'manners', or culture as we might call it today, which form the matrix of all power, contract, authority and legality. Culture is the sediment in which power settles and takes root. Burke comments:

> Manners are of more importance than laws. Upon them, in a great measure, the law depends . . . Manners are what vex or soothe, corrupt or purify, exalt or debase, barbarise or refine us, by a constant, steady, uniform, insensible operation, like that of the air we breathe. They give the whole form and colour to our lives.[22]

It is not only manners in the sense of social graces that Burke has in mind, but the time-honoured customs and convictions by which men and women live. Manners in this sense are also an abiding concern of Burke's contemporary Jane Austen, for whom abstract moral precepts are made acceptable, even agreeable, by being lived out with style and vivacity. The two elder Bennet sisters of *Pride and Prejudice* are highly moral women, but gracefully, engagingly so. They unite the ethical with the aesthetic, a condition which the censorious Mr Knightley of *Emma* fails to achieve. There are characters like

Maria Crawford in *Mansfield Park* whose vitality gets the better of their morality, and others like Fanny Price in the same novel who (partly on account of the Maria Crawfords of this world) are forced to sacrifice social style to moral principle.

Burke believes that political power must be similarly aestheticised, made gratifying and pleasurable, if it is to engage the loyalties of the common people. An authority that fails in this task will be more feared than loved, and its hold over the populace is thus likely to be precarious:

> Public affections, combined with manners, are required sometimes as supplements, sometimes as correctives, always as aids to law. There ought to be a system of manners in every nation which a well-formed mind would be disposed to relish. To make us love our county, our country ought to be lovely.[23]

Once power has been alchemised into culture, dissolved into the texture of our everyday conduct, we can all come to be pleasantly oblivious of the coercive instruments it holds in reserve; and since we will then submit spontaneously to its commands, it will find no need to deploy them.

If Burke is repelled by the French Revolution, it is largely because he regards it as the ruin of this whole project. As the tumbrils roll up to the guillotine, the instruments of coercion in Paris are starkly on show. He writes wrathfully of the Jacobins:

All the pleasing illusions which made power gentle, and obedience liberal, which harmonised the different shades of life, and which, by a bland assimilation, incorporate into politics the sentiments which beautify and soften private society, are to be dissolved by the new conquering empire of light and reason. All the decent drapery of life is to be rudely torn off.[24]

The Revolution is as much an assault on aesthetics as an onslaught on morals. It is no wonder that in Burke's eyes it is such a tawdry affair, all cheap farce, windy bombast and maladroit melodrama. Power, in his view, works by fiction and charade, cloaking itself in ceremony in order to soften its rigour. It wins our devotion by writing its obligations on the heart. Yet it is this faith that fiction is integral to the social order that the French revolutionaries impiously spurn. In Burke's view, they are crazed enough to believe that society can work by reason alone. They also labour under the delusion that power is most effective when it is most on show. The truth, however, is that nobody can gaze on the nakedness of the Law and live, which is why it needs the fig leaf of what Gramsci will later call hegemony.

Burke's dismay at the tumultuous events across the Channel, then, is more than the panic of one pledged to church and crown. It springs from his conviction that the very principle of hegemony, or rule by consent, has been wantonly abandoned. It is as though the French, intoxicated by an abstract Reason, have made a catastrophic blunder about the very nature of politics. Their uprising is not just an outbreak of civilised savagery but a dissolution of civil society as such, and thus of the very condition of effective governance. There can be no government through the affections in revolutionary France, only hacked and mutilated bodies. Untempered by custom and sensibility, Reason has run riot, and the result is a general madness.

Burke therefore deplores the Jacobins on much the same grounds as he castigates the Ascendancy in Ireland and British colonialism in India and America. In none of these cases, he considers, do the rulers seek to accommodate themselves to the culture of the ruled, adapting their sovereignty to age-old pieties and sentiments. Politics, he remarks, 'requires a deep knowledge of human nature and human necessities . . . The nature of man is intricate; the objects of society are of the greatest possible complexity; and therefore no simple disposition or direction of power can be suitable either to man's nature, or to the quality of his affairs.'[25] He is, he confesses, unable to judge a situation 'on a simple view of the object as it stands stripped of every relation', since it is 'circumstance . . . which gives in reality to every political principle its distinguishing colour, and discriminating effect'.[26] The complexity Burke has in mind – the unfathomable specificity of human affairs – is what we know as culture, even if he himself did not use the word in this sense. It is this intricate mesh of affinities and observances that power ignores at its peril.

Burke rejects the modern distinction between private affections and public utility. He is reluctant to confine feeling to the domestic sphere, leaving the public realm to the tender mercies of law, contract and impersonal obligation. We should treat the faults of the state as we would 'the wounds of a father, with pious awe and trembling solicitude'.[27] 'We have given to the frame of our polity', he observes, 'the image of a relation in blood, binding up the constitution of our country with the dearest domestic ties; adopting our fundamental laws into the bosom of our family affections'.[28] As an Irishman, he was familiar with the so-called moral economy of the Irish countryside, in which custom, tradition and sentiment could accrue the force of legal right. To transplant this situation to the metropolitan society into which he was adopted meant governing with regard to popular prejudice and customary expectations. Burke would heartily have endorsed Friedrich Schiller's complaint that 'the [modern] state remains for ever a stranger to its citizens since at no point does it ever make contact with their feeling'.[29]

There is, to be sure, a large dose of self-interest at stake here. Burke is well aware that to win hearts and minds is the surest way to prevent political disaffection. The real danger to every state, he observes, 'is to render its subjects justly discontented'.[30] If the colonies associate their own liberty with your sovereignty, they will cling to you faithfully. Obedience will follow hard on the heels of love. Yet Burke's refusal to expel feeling from the public realm, his insistence that interests and affections are the seedbed of politics, also anticipates some modern feminist thought, dismayed though he would have been to hear it. Women, in his view, were to be venerated rather than liberated.

If culture is what sweetens your authority and renders it tolerable, then it is an indispensable medium of political power. That power needs to bed itself down in everyday experience, cloak itself in the garments of common loyalties, if it is not to loom up as abstract and intimidating. If it appears too daunting and aloof, it is in danger of alienating the very citizens it seeks to grapple to it. Burke was an aesthetician as well as a politician, and writes in his treatise on aesthetics on the terrifying nature of the sublime, as opposed to the pleasurable, harmonious character of the beautiful.[31] It is not hard to translate this antithesis into a political one. The Law itself is sublime, a kind of virile 'swelling', and like the nakedness of the father is terrible to look on; so that to beguile us into falling in love with it, it must become a cross-dresser, concealing its brutality by decking itself out in seductive feminine dress. Burke is aware that our relationship to authority has a smack of Oedipal ambivalence about it: as chronic masochists, we delight in being cowed by the implacable Name of the Father at the same time as we chafe against it. The problem, however, is that our very veneration for this august figure 'hinders us from having that entire love for him that we have for our mothers, where the parental authority is almost melted down into the mother's fondness and indulgence'.[32] The danger, then, is that the law we respect we do not love, and the law we love we do not respect. An equipoise must therefore be struck between the paternal and maternal, coercion and consent. Power must be made gratifying, but not to the point where it dispels the awe and deference of its subjects. Its feminine garments must be diaphanous enough to hint at the bulge of the phallus beneath them.

There is a narrational aspect to this shift from masculine to feminine. Burke has no Lockeian illusions about the peaceable foundation of the state. On the contrary, he believes that most political states were founded by violence, invasion, revolution or usurpation. Their origins are thus illicit, and only the gradual passage of time can draw a veil over these bloodstained beginnings. In the beginning was coercion, which later modulates into consent. Your landed estate is mine if I stole it from you a long enough time ago. If I purloined it only last week, then you have the right to demand it back. The longer a nation survives, the more acceptable its sovereignty becomes, which is one reason why states born in bloodshed within living memory (such as Israel), or almost within living memory (such as Northern Ireland), have an acute problem of legitimation. Effective power rests on collective amnesia, as crimes come to grow on us like old cronies. 'Time alone gives solidity to [the rulers'] right', comments David Hume in his

Treatise of Human Nature, 'and operating gradually on the minds of men, reconciles them to any authority, and makes it seem just and reasonable.'[33] Legitimacy is longevity. Power is founded on oblivion. It is time above all that will convert the primordial trespass into a legality to be revered.

It is history, then, that converts politics into that second nature we call culture, habituating us to what might once have appeared intolerable. 'Time', Burke writes, 'has, by degrees ... blended and coalited the conquered with the conquerors'[34] – though by no means everywhere, he considers, and certainly not in Ireland and India. Nations, like individuals for Freud, flourish by repressing the trauma of their origin, thrusting it into the political unconscious. It is just this that the Jacobins have failed to do. In their metaphysical frenzy they have inquired too deeply into things, stripping off the decorous vestments of culture, laying bare the shameful sources of social existence and turning their impious gaze on the father's phallus. Yet nobody can look upon this sublime authority without being struck blind; and in the case of the French revolutionaries, this blindness is the bedazzlement which comes from an excess of light. For Burke, the name of that light is Reason. An excess of Reason is a form of madness, as Burke's compatriots Jonathan Swift and Laurence Sterne were also aware.

All power betrays a degree of humbug. Those who govern are conscious of the arbitrary, unfounded nature of their authority, but seek to persuade their subjects otherwise. In this process, culture or aesthetics – revered customs, the glamour of aristocracy, the sacred aura of kingship, the pomp of parliament – is of key importance. Burke's whole cultural project is to refute the claim that the emperor has no clothes. Instead, power must beguile the senses, breeding salutary fictions and edifying illusions. It is uplift and consolation the common people need, not truth, and only a society well-practised in the uses of symbol and ceremony can provide them. If the state is to thrive, it must turn itself into a work of art.

Yet there is another aspect to the situation. Culture for Burke may be an instrument of power, but it is also a terrain on which power can be contested. If it is the cement of the social formation, it is also its potential point of fracture. In one sense, culture would appear the opposite of politics. Politics is a matter of practical issues, conscious calculations, the cut-and-thrust of the contemporary, whereas culture in the Burkeian sense of the term inhabits an almost geologically slow time, one of gradually sedimented affections and aversions which prove resistant to abrupt change. It is a question of unbroken continuities of place, language, kinship, belief and community, and as such figures among other things as a right-wing bulwark against left-wing revolution. It is by no means an inherently radical notion. In fact, if one were asked to name one major reason for the rise of the concept of culture in early nineteenth-century Europe, one might do worse than reply: the French Revolution. It was against such political tumult that the idea was wielded. Yet, as Burke recognises, with his own colonial background well in mind, culture can be a spur to revolution as well as an antidote to it. Nothing in his view is more likely to lead to social upheaval than a high-handed disregard for the time-hallowed customs of a people. Culture and tradition can thus be disruptive forces as well as preservative ones. A case which is conservative when applied to metropolitan nations can be radical in the context of the colonies. It is this that Burke's right-wing admirers fail to register. It was also a fact to which most of his colleagues at Westminster were blind, given that few of them laboured under the disadvantage of being Irish. (One notable exception was the playwright and Member of Parliament Richard Sheridan, a man who for a time practised the admirable duplicity of being both a British government minister and a fellow-traveller with the revolutionary United Irishmen.)

The idea of culture as the opposite of politics – as a higher, purer realm than horse-trading and vote-fixing – belongs to the lineage of so-called *Kulturkritik*, for which the life of the spirit is not to be tainted by mere utility.[35] *Kulturkritik* severs culture from politics, while the cultural politics of our own day is in danger of reducing the one to the other. Burke himself pursues neither of these projects. In his view, culture and politics are to be neither divided nor conflated. It is necessary instead to grasp the complex relations between them, as well as to acknowledge the truth that this is not a relation between equals. In the end, it is culture that has the upper hand.

* * *

The German philosopher Johann Gottfried Herder was Edmund Burke's contemporary, and an author whose importance in the history of ideas is hard to overrate. He was one of the first great historicist thinkers, attentive to the historical circumstances of cultures, texts, events and individuals. It is an approach which has been described as one of the great intellectual revolutions of European thought.[36] He has also been hailed as the father of modern nationalism, and has even been credited with introducing the idea of culture as a whole way of life into European thought. As if all this were not impressive enough, Herder was also one of the founders of modern literary theory, as well as one of the first thinkers to recognise the role of popular culture in social life. As such, he stands at the source of what we know today as cultural studies. He was also a pioneer in the philosophy of language, a subject which some credit him with having effectively invented. The philosopher Charles Taylor claims that Herder 'originates a fundamentally different way of thinking about language and meaning', and speaks of 'the Herder revolution'.[37]

Despite these achievements, Herder's name is less familiar in Anglophone circles than that of his Irish counterpart. The fact that the Nazis revered him as a racist is no doubt one reason for this relative neglect, though he was for the most part no more of a racist than Burke was a reactionary. It is true that like a good many thinkers of his time, including the great liberal Immanuel Kant, he believed that some races were more advanced than others, and occasionally deployed demeaning stereotypes of those he considered backward or childlike. Unlike the Nazis, however, he did not consider that such peoples were any less entitled to their full human rights, including the right to be neither colonised nor enslaved.

Herder and Burke do not always think alike. Herder, for example, greeted the French Revolution with acclaim, though like many an initial enthusiast he was later to be disillusioned. Whereas Burke treats women with old-style chivalry, Herder speaks up boldly for their emancipation, announcing that 'no fact shows more decisively the true character of a man or a nation than their treatment of women'.[38] Most women, he believes, are slaves within their own societies. If Burke prizes order, Herder values freedom. Burke's vision of humankind can be dark, while Herder's is far too sanguine. There is no such thing as evil, he proclaims, and death is merely a metamorphosis. History is the work of God. Burke is rather less dewy-eyed about the evolution of humanity. In the Irishman's view, the political state is to be revered, whereas in the German's eyes it is a heartless administrative machine which suppresses all individuality. The true makers of history are the poets and prophets, not the politicians.

Even so, there are some striking affinities between the two men. Herder, like Burke, holds that culture is more decisive

than politics. Both men see religion as central to culture –
unsurprisingly in the case of Herder, who was a Lutheran
minister. Ideas are the province of the intelligentsia, but religion is a species of emotional democracy, a treasure-house of
instincts and affections accessible to all. Both writers thought
that nations are to be governed through customs, traditions
and sentiments, and society must be seen as an organic growth.
As such, it resists the kind of centralised organisation that
Burke abhors in French Jacobinism and Herder finds distasteful
in German absolutism. Both men are Romantics wedded to
the concrete and circumstantial, yet both refuse to give way on
certain universal standards. At the same time, they are at one
in decrying what they regard as a bogus cult of universal
humanitarianism, as opposed to local loyalties and domestic
bonds. 'Ideals of universal love of humanity, for all nations,
and even enemies, are exalted', Herder complains of the spirit
of the age, 'while warm feelings of family and friendship are
allowed to decay.'[39] Sympathy and love, for him as for Burke,
are more precious than what he dismisses as 'cold reason'.

Herder shares Burke's hatred of slavery, despotism, colonial rapacity and the destruction of native cultures. Like his
Irish counterpart, he champions the cause of small nations
and warns the imperialist powers of Europe that they are
likely one day to get their comeuppance. 'The more means
and tools we Europeans invent to enslave, cheat and plunder
you other continents', he remarks, addressing himself to the

77

subjects of colonial power, 'the more it may be left to you to triumph in the end. We forge the chains by which one day you will pull us along.'[40] Europe, he insists, should not seek to mould its colonies into pallid replicas of itself. Instead, the culture of other nations must be respected, since each of them contributes in its distinctive way to the universal development of humanity.[41] 'Is good not dispersed over the earth?' he asks.[42] To grasp the unique character of other peoples, one needs to suspend one's partiality and grasp their form of life from the inside, rather as Burke believed of India. 'It is but just, when we proceed to the country of the blacks', Herder insists, 'that we lay aside our proud prejudices, and consider the organisation of this quarter of the globe with as much impartiality as if there were no other.'[43]

Herder, then, is far from the rampant German nationalist the Nazis claimed to see in him. Yet neither is he a full-blooded cultural relativist, at least in his later writings. He would have been unenthused by the coy refusal to criticise 'the other' which marks so much contemporary postcolonial thought, and which can simply be a shamefaced inversion of colonial values. Instead, he is not in the least reluctant to pass negative judgements on a whole span of human cultures, from the ancient Romans to the modern Tibetans. These assessments are sometimes coloured by racism or ethnocentrism, and sometimes not. Some nations are superior to others in particular respects; but no culture is inferior or superior as such, and none of them has the right to behave aggressively or expansively towards others. Far from being a self-satisfied European, Herder holds that the continent has been in a lamentable state of decay ever since the Middle Ages, and is in need of radical cultural renewal. It is a civilisation, to be sure; but it has lost touch with its vital cultural roots, a calamity which Herder's own work sets out to repair. His project, along with that of many another Romantic, is to convert civilisations into cultures.

Herder believes in the perfectibility of the human species. Civilisation can regress from time to time, but taken as a whole it is evolving towards a state of universal well-being. Yet he combines this Enlightenment optimism with a rejection of the standard Enlightenment view of progress. History for Herder is by no means a single, uniform, unilinear process of evolution; rather, each culture unfolds at its own pace in its own inimitable way. The idea of progress is pluralised. At the same time, the notion of culture as *Bildung* or harmonious self-development is transferred from the individual to entire nations. Herder sees the spiritual evolution of these nations as a value in itself, not simply as a contribution to some universal march towards utopia. The point, as one critic comments, is 'not to trace the trajectory of "progress" but to discriminate the varieties of human excellence'.[44] There is no inexorable teleology at work here. 'You people in all parts of the world,' Herder announces, 'who have passed away over the ages, you did not live only to fertilize the earth with your ashes, so that at the end of time your descendants could become happy through European culture.'[45] Non-Western communities are more than sacrificial lambs to be lain on the altar of universal improvement. Nor is history a one-way street: there is much that the present can learn from the supposedly benighted past. For Herder, as for Marx, civilisation involves both loss and gain, and some degree of decline is a function of all social advance.

Both Herder and Burke maintain that reason is rooted in felt experience. Cognition and sensation are on intimate terms with one other. Among other things, this means that power, which depends upon concepts, must be grounded in culture, which is an experiential affair. As one concerned not primarily with art but with perception and sensation, Burke is an aesthetician in the original sense of the word. In fact, modern aesthetics begins as a discourse of the body.[46] In his treatise on the sublime and the beautiful, he is fascinated by what happens when we hear low vibrations or stroke smooth surfaces, by the dilation of the eye's pupil in darkness or the feel of a slight tap on the shoulder. Herder, too, believes that thought is bound up with the body, and that language is affective and expressive rather than simply communicative. A slight change in human physiology, he claims, would transform the destiny of the planet. For Burke, too, language is a question of performance rather than conveyance, rhetoric rather than reportage. It is a view exemplified by his magnificent prose style, laced as it is with burnished metaphor and theatrical gesture.

In viewing language as bound up with our social and sensory activity, Herder anticipates the thought of both Nietzsche and Wittgenstein. For him, as for Wittgenstein, words have meaning only in so far as they are woven into a practical form of life. It is because of language that we can inhabit different worlds even when we live on the same street. Speech is an organ with which we cope with our practical environment, and all of our more abstract notions evolve from this humble root. Pure reason is a chimera. Like Burke, Herder promotes faith, sense, experience and intuition over rational speculation. In fact, he has the nerve to criticise his great mentor Kant for underestimating the role of language in the process of cognition, as well as for failing to anchor the categories of time and space in bodily experience. To insert language into the Kantian system, he argues, would be to throw it open to the forces of history and culture. Like Burke, too, he is impatient with philosophical system-building, though his work is far more ambitious in scope than the Irishman's, ranging as it does from the grunting of the ape to the structure of the cosmos. He even modestly contemplated writing a history of the world.

In the field of language, Herder is probably best known for the doctrine that language and thought are inseparable – a case which he did not originate but which he did much to advance.

The view of the Bakhtin school that all discourse is dialogical, and that thought is a kind of inner speech, is already to be found in the dense thicket of Herder's writings. Perhaps the time has come to raise a few unseasonable doubts about this most received of theoretical positions. If cultural theorists were to spend more time playing with their infants or frolicking with their pets, they might come to see that these speechless creatures ('infant' means 'speechless one') are nonetheless capable of something that looks inconveniently like thought. A dog can figure out that since the cat is now perched high in the tree it might as well turn its mind to more fruitful pursuits, just as a toddler may be aware that its mother's absence is only temporary. It is true that dogs cannot be Southern Baptists or toddlers neo-Darwinists, a fact which indeed has much to do with their lack of language. A sign-system of some kind is essential for these more complex cultural activities, which do not depend so crucially on the body. But it is not clear that a toddler needs to be able to articulate the words 'I'm just going to cough myself into a frenzy in order to distract my mother's attention from that damned baby' in order to be able to think it. Nor does a toddler need to think to itself 'If I put my foot on the toy car it will stop rolling in the wrong direction.' There is a kind of practical or somatic intelligence at work here which does service for some more articulate form of discourse.

Like many who followed in his wake, Herder considers language to be the decisive factor in human culture. Though he grants that all languages are hybrid, made up of the scraps and leavings of other tongues, he sees the unity of a mode of speech as reflecting the unity of a nation. 'To imagine a language', Ludwig Wittgenstein was later to write in his *Philosophical Investigations* (§19) 'is to imagine a form of life.' In Herder's view, every language gives voice to the distinctive world-view of a specific people; and though there can be many a cross-fertilisation between such linguistic communities, it is their singularity which he prizes above all. There is a rich diversity of cultures, but each of them is best viewed as an integral whole. Internal plurality is generally undesirable. In fact, one of Herder's complaints against colonialism is that it mongrelises a previously unadulterated nation. If he detests slavery, it is partly because it rips men and women from their native soil and transplants them to other cultures, a hybridisation which may then cause them to degenerate. Nations are the natural unit of humanity. Since Herder looks to a federal alliance of such units, he is by no means a German chauvinist; but though the migration of peoples is unavoidable, and an internationalist outlook is to be acclaimed, he would probably have agreed with T.S. Eliot's pontifical pronouncement that 'on the whole, it would appear to be for the best that the great majority of human beings go on living in the place in which they were born'.[47] (Eliot himself was brought up in St. Louis, Missouri, became a postgraduate student in Oxford, travelled a good deal in continental Europe and spent the rest of his life in London.)

A culture is at its finest for Herder when its language artic-
ulates the vital stuff of popular experience. It is a view to be
found as late as the work of F.R. Leavis. Language begins life
as a kind of poetry, ripe, robust and richly flavoured, but grows
enervated and anaemic the more civilisation declines into
empty refinement – or, in a word, into Frenchness. Meanwhile,
colonialism transforms the material conditions of a people,
and in doing so plunders their language of its vital substance.
It can even rob them of their native tongue, thereby divesting
them of their very experience. The Irish nationalist leader
Thomas Davis complains that:

> to impose another language on . . . a people is to send
> their history adrift among the accidents of translation –
> 'tis to tear their identity from all places – 'tis to substitute
> arbitrary signs for picturesque and suggestive names – 'tis
> to cut off the entail of feeling, and separate the people
> from their forefathers by a deep gulf.[48]

Language and culture distil the spiritual biography of a
people, and grow brittle once its unique savour is dulled and
staled.

What will restore language to its pristine state of health,
Herder maintained, is the life of the common people. It is
as though the middle and upper classes stand for civilisation,
while the folk themselves represent culture. Unknown to

themselves, these half-famished peasants and fatigued factory hands constitute a storehouse of timeless wisdom. Germany must accordingly turn from Racine, Goethe and an insipid neo-classicism to the purity, vigour and simplicity of folk art. It is the *Volk* who will redeem a civilisation half-dead at the top. The animal vitality of the masses will rejuvenate a jaded society. Culture is in this sense an internal critique of civilisation. 'What did courts and academies, libraries and galleries ever do for the education of the country, the people, the subjects?' Herder asks scornfully.[49] Folk song is of course quite as artificial as Wagnerian opera, and the very notion of the *Volk* is an invention of middle-class intellectuals; but Herder was convinced that the art of Homer, Sophocles and Shakespeare was nourished by the popular culture of its day, and that this perpetual source of creative energy must again be tapped in his own time. It is as though popular culture represents the collective unconscious on which individual artists may draw.

The fable and song of the past, then, will lay the foundation of the future. It is to a native literature that the task of nation-building must be entrusted. The arts are once more to become public phenomena, social interventions rather than idle amusements. Aesthetics must be subordinated to ethics, civilisation to culture, the artificial to the spontaneous, the written word to the living voice and the upper classes to the common people. Herder's project combines a number of different senses of the word 'culture': culture as the arts must be nurtured by culture as a distinctive form of life (that of the populace), so that culture in the sense of civilisation as a whole may be reclaimed. For Burke, power must woo the culture of the people; for Herder at his most militant, it must abdicate and allow that way of life to reign in its stead. If the people are to come into their own, the state must wither away.

* * *

Few thinkers might appear more remote from Herder's Romantic populism than the mandarin figure of T.S. Eliot. Yet Eliot, who was a fan of jazz and music hall, is in his own patrician way as much preoccupied with popular culture as his German counterpart, whatever the yawning political gulf between the two. As with Burke, the word 'culture' for Eliot signifies in the first place the social unconscious. It means 'the *whole way of life* of a people, from birth to the grave, from morning to night and even in sleep',[50] but this way of life is not one of which we can ever be fully aware. A culture, Eliot comments, 'can never be wholly conscious – there is always more to it than we are conscious of; and it cannot be planned because it is always the unconscious background of all our planning'.[51] In Heideggerian terms, culture represents the set of pre-understandings or primordial orientation to the world which render our thought and action possible in the first place, and so will always elude our grasp as a whole. In Lacanian parlance, it is the field of the Other within which any specific other can be seen to emerge.

It is worth noting the slide here from Eliot's claim that culture can never be wholly conscious to the assertion that it can never be planned. If it can be conscious to some extent, as he seems to imply, then some degree of planning would surely seem possible. The fact that we cannot scrutinise all our most deep-seated assumptions all of the time (since some of them will constitute the taken-for-granted context of the scrutinising) does not prevent us from rolling out a regional arts policy or organising a national rail system. As a conservative opponent of state intervention and social engineering, Eliot shifts rather deviously here from a philosophical claim to a tacitly political one. He is thereby in danger of selling the ideological pass in the opposite direction, making culture appear too deterministic a phenomenon. If we are shaped to the core by these profoundly unconscious forces, in what sense can we be responsible for ourselves? And what price then our religious faith or royalist convictions?

It may come as a surprise that Eliot, an Anglo-Catholic conservative who holds that the great majority of men and women are incapable of genuine thought, declares himself strongly in favour of a common culture. The case appears less curious once one recognises that a common culture in his view would by no means be an egalitarian one. All citizens will participate in the same form of life, but they will do so in notably unequal ways. The same culture will be lived out unconsciously by the common people and self-consciously by the minority. A coterie of intellectuals will brood over fundamental truths, while the great majority of men and women will adhere to some version of these values without being aware that they do. Instead, they will live them out spontaneously, in their everyday conduct and ritual observance. Indeed, if ordinary people are to live by spiritual values while being incapable of much self-reflection, this unconscious form of fine living would seem unavoidable. Besides, too much cold-eyed conceptual analysis might play havoc with their spontaneous loyalties and allegiances. Culture, bemusingly, is both the subtlest kind of knowledge and what we know but don't need to know that we do. Rather as you can be a haemophiliac without being aware of it, so you can be profoundly cultured while being entirely ignorant of the fact. There can, however, be no question of consciously extending the values of the minority to the populace as a whole, since 'to aim to make everyone share in the appreciation of the fruits of the more conscious part of the culture is to adulterate and cheapen what you give'.[52]

The social order Eliot has in mind would be of a Christian persuasion, in which a secular priesthood of intellectuals and the more socially conscientious upper classes would preside benevolently over the simple faithful. It is true that by the time he came to propose this ideal, religious faith had been losing ground with the masses for at least a century. Even so, it would be hard to lay the foundations of such a community without religious faith, since few other cultural forms are shared by elite and populace alike, and those that both prelates and plumbers do happen to have in common lack the necessary spiritual depth. Cricket, or an admiration for the consummate artistry of 'The Teddy Bears' Picnic', are unlikely to provide the cement of the social order.

Burke, as we have seen, wishes to preserve an elitist culture, but is convinced that it must be responsive to the pieties of the populace if it is to survive. Herder, more subversively, calls on the civilisation of the governors to yield to the culture of the governed. Eliot's case is more complex. Unlike Herder, he does not elevate popular culture over the art of a coterie; instead, he is intent on forging a bond between the two. He is not out to replace high art with legend and folklore, but to allow that art to be fed by such fertile resources, and thus to rediscover its roots in the social unconscious. In fact, this would not be a bad description of *The Waste Land*, a piece of minority culture that nonetheless draws upon myths and motifs plucked from the so-called collective unconscious. This is why Eliot, rather absurdly, claims that he would prefer his readers to be semi-literate, for all the formidable difficulty of his work. A semi-literate reader, one innocently undistracted by intellectual matters, is likely to be more receptive to the unconscious implications of his poetry. He is relatively indifferent to the question of whether his readers are alert to his abstruse allusions, since his poetry goes stealthily to work on them at a much less conceptual level. Indeed, he himself claimed to have enjoyed reading Dante before he could understand a word of Italian. One must read with one's guts and nerve-endings rather than with one's mind. As with Burke and Herder, thinking is a bodily affair. At the conscious level, minority and mass cultures must be kept rigorously apart, lest extending the former to the latter results in its dilution and decay; but there can be a sort of subliminal traffic between the two spheres, as what one might call the articulate dimension of a culture (its religious doctrines, for example) infiltrates the communal unconscious, which in turn surreptitiously shapes its more explicit values.

Most cultural theorists today reject elites as divorced from the common life. They caricature the case they dismiss and underestimate the deviousness of its advocates. Like most astute elitists, Eliot recognises that minority values are unlikely to flourish unless they implant themselves in commonly shared soil. It is an insight he shares with fascism. A constant circulation of energy can thus be set up between two senses of culture: as the work of a coterie, and as a whole way of life. The higher level of culture, Eliot argues, 'must be thought of both as valuable in itself, and as an enrichment of the lower levels: thus the movement of culture would proceed in a kind of cycle, each class nourishing the others'.[53] Maintaining 'a high level of culture', he writes, 'is to the benefit not merely of the class that maintains it but to society as a whole'.[54] The masses, in short, will reap value from minority culture without being aware of the fact, rather as one might benefit from a change in the interest rate or a more ruthlessly amoral Secret Intelligence Service without knowing that you do. It is not clear how farm labourers profit from the fact that a small handful of their fellow citizens appreciate the music of Webern, or (in a wider sense of culture) from the fact that they send their children to expensive private schools; but it is edifying to know that engaging in such activities is in some obscure sense philanthropic. In working on one's history of Charles the Bald, one is somehow enhancing the existence of men and women who have never even heard of him.

The enrichment is two-way, however, since the poet and scholar then cease to be solitary figures. They can now claim pivotal status in the culture as a whole. The task of the intelligentsia is to give supremely articulate expression to the collective mind of the people, not simply to their own private musings. W.B. Yeats, for example, saw his poetry as giving voice to the myths and archetypes of the Irish peasantry. Rather as it is not Eliot who speaks in *The Waste Land*, but what he himself rather grandly calls the European mind, so Yeats is simply a medium, almost in the spiritualistic sense, for the timeless wisdom of the populace. For Martin Heidegger, somewhat more sinisterly, the poet's task is to lend his tongue to the destiny of the nation. There are jobs for artists once more. In a modernist age in which some of them have been forced into solitude and exile, it is comforting to imagine that they can still speak of more than themselves.

There have been a good many commentators for whom a central task of the critic is to defend minority culture from the infection of the masses.[55] Eliot, however, takes a different view, largely because the masses he has in mind are a mythical Christian peasantry rather than a real-life godless proletariat. Like many a modernist, his aim is to couple elitism and primitivism. The civilised and the elemental must enter into mutual dialogue. The sophisticate must go to school with the savage. Or, to put it another way, the deracinated intellectual must find a home among the common people. Eliot was an exile from his own country, and exiles are especially likely to romanticise the idea of rootedness. Indeed, this may be one reason for the early Eliot's anti-Semitism, since Jews are traditionally regarded as homeless wanderers, and thus present the intellectual vagrant with a distasteful image of his own condition. Like some other modernists (Joyce and Pound spring especially to mind), Eliot could rationalise his own deracination by discovering a deep-seated mythological unity at the very heart of civilisation, a spiritual nation of which outcasts like himself could be loyal citizens.

* * *

If there is a conservative case for culture as the social unconscious, there is a radical version of it as well. Both positions, as we have seen, are present in the writings of Burke, but the radical case can also be found in Raymond Williams's *Culture and Society 1780–1950*:

A culture, while it is being lived, is always in part unknown, in part unrealised. The making of a community is always an exploration, for consciousness cannot precede creation, and there is no formula for unknown experience. A good community, a living culture, will, because of this, not only make room for but actively encourage all and any who can contribute to the advance in consciousness which is the common need . . . We need to consider every attachment, every value, with our whole attention; for we do not know the future, we may never be certain of what may enrich it.[56]

Unlike Eliot, Williams links the social unconscious to the fact that a culture is always a work in progress. If it can never be dredged fully to consciousness, it is partly because it is never complete. The unconscious of a culture is thus among other things an effect of its historicity. It is the future that we cannot know, not simply the concealed subtext of our contemporary thought and action; and for this reason we can never be sure which cultural strains in the present will prove fruitful, and which will turn out to be culs-de-sac. Eliot, by contrast, is confident of which values are to be affirmed, and does not need to wait upon the future to find out. Historicity, then, is one reason why, in Williams's view, a culture can never be totalised. But it is also because any modern social order, unlike Eliot's homogeneous, largely rural community, is in his view likely to be 'a very complex system of specialised developments – the whole of which will form the whole culture, but which will not be available, or conscious as a whole, to any individual or group living within it'.[57] What will be conscious for some will not be so for others; but this is not, as it is with Eliot, a question of whether you are a landowner or a poacher. For Williams, the conscious and unconscious dimensions of a culture are not hierarchically distributed, but aspects of a single project.

A common culture for the conservative Eliot is one which is commonly shared, while for the socialist Williams it is one which is commonly made. Williams's common culture is thus both more and less conscious than Eliot's: more so, because it involves the active participation of all its members; less so, because what will emerge from this unfathomably intricate collaboration can be neither drafted in advance nor fully transparent in the making. If this lack of transparency is true for Eliot, it is even more the case for Williams, since the more agents are actively at work in the construction of a culture, the less the effects of their actions can be grasped as a whole. We can leave him with the final word on the question:

> We have to plan what can be planned, according to our common decision. But the emphasis of the idea of culture

is right when it reminds us that a culture, essentially, is unplannable. We have to ensure the means of life, and the means of community. But what will then, by these means, be lived, we cannot know or say.[58]

* * *

So far we have looked at a number of issues in the theory of culture. Culture can be a model of how to live, a form of self-fashioning or self-realisation, the fruit of a coterie or the life-form of a whole people, a critique of the present or an image of the future. For an author in whose life and work all of these themes converge, we can turn now by way of summary to the thought of Oscar Wilde.

CHAPTER FOUR

An Apostle of Culture

LIKE HIS COMPATRIOT Edmund Burke, Oscar Wilde was educated at Trinity College, Dublin and later made a splash in London. Both men were much preoccupied with art. Burke, as we have seen, was the author of a treatise on aesthetics which has a bearing on political questions, while Wilde was a flamboyant aesthete whose devotion to art for art's sake, as we shall see in a moment, was among other things a devious form of political radicalism. At a conservative arithmetical estimate, both authors led double lives. Burke was an eminent Westminster politician who in the course of his high-flying career in England kept much of his Irish provenance a close secret. His family in Ireland had Catholic connections, about which he was understandably sensitive. In fact, a distant relation of his, a Catholic priest, had been hanged, drawn and quartered by the British as a political rebel. It was not the kind of subject one would readily bring up in the London coffee houses. Wilde was both socialite and sodomite, upper class and underdog, respectable citizen and hirer of rent boys, a shameless *bon viveur* who laid claim to the title of socialist. His very name yokes the Gaelic 'Oscar' to the English 'Wilde', linking a mythological Irish hero to the world of middle-class drawing rooms. If he hobnobbed with the Lady Bracknells, he also moved at ease in insurrectionary circles, counting revolutionaries like William Morris and Peter Kropotkin among his friends.

Both Wilde and Burke were master-rhetoricians legendary for their verbal élan, and as Irish émigrés in England both ended up biting the hand that fed them. They were also akin in their distaste for British colonialism. Though Burke was not hostile to the colonial venture as such, he felt some solidarity with anti-British rebels in Ireland and America and arraigned a prominent English colonial official, Warren Hastings, before the House of Commons. For his part, Wilde satirised the very English upper classes into whose ranks he had smuggled himself as a sort of fifth columnist. His sparkling stage comedy is both impeccably conventional and secretly subversive. He was a socialist and Irish republican, the son of a mother who was a celebrated feminist and nationalist rebel, and a father who was a distinguished Irish scholar and patriot. With his usual contrariness, however, he believed that Ireland should govern England rather than vice versa. The two émigrés were both to fall prey to Britain's contempt for its longest-standing colonial subjects. Burke was sneered at as a Paddy, while Wilde was imprisoned for bedding a sprig of the English aristocracy whose filial duty was to reproduce his ancestral line rather than to consort with exotic gay foreigners.

Both Irishmen felt compassion for the poor and dispossessed, perhaps feeling themselves to be more fortunate examples of such outcasts. The Irish writer adrift in London and subject to racial abuse was a higher version of the immigrant road-builder or railway worker. Wilde once gave away his coat to a beggar on London Bridge. Both kinds of immigrant had been forced out of their native land by its chronic impoverishment – material in the case of the road-builder, cultural in the case of the writers. In V.S. Naipaul's phrase, the latter were 'mimic men', imitating the English gentry (Wilde was careful to shed his Irish brogue while at Oxford) while covertly or openly dissenting from their view of the world. Both thinkers held in different ways to the constitutive role of fiction in social existence. In London, Wilde adopted a persona assumed by a lineage of other Irish literary immigrants to the city from Oliver Goldsmith to Brendan Behan, that of licensed jester to the English Establishment. Yet, as another such Irish jester, George Bernard Shaw, warned, it was a perilous role to perform. One had to be careful not to get too big for one's boots lest the natives cut one savagely down to size, and prudence was never Wilde's most conspicuous virtue. Five years before his downfall, the English had hounded another Anglo-Irishman, the nationalist leader Charles Stewart Parnell, this time over a heterosexual rather than homosexual scandal, forcing him into a political wilderness where he was to die a broken man one year later. Both Wilde and Parnell were first courted and admired, then thrust out into the cold as immoralists. What his persecutors failed to grasp was that if Wilde was gay, it was among other things because he found heterosexuality so intolerably clichéd. Indeed, he was the kind of man who would almost have preferred to fall foul of the English judicial system than fall victim to a stereotype. His whole life was one long unnatural practice.

Wilde came from the city which James Joyce, a later Dublin émigré, spelt as 'Doublin', and almost everything about him was doubled, divided, ambiguous. It was a matter of 'two thinks at a time', as Joyce puts it in *Finnegans Wake*. A truth in art, Wilde declared, is one whose opposite is also true, and much the same can be said of his own brilliant, blighted career. The self-division is there in that creature of the Wildean imagination Dorian Gray, behind whose smooth-featured appearance a dreadful secret is festering. Wilde's best-known play, *The Importance of Being Earnest*, is all about secret codes, split identities and shady origins, stacking illusion upon illusion and sceptical of any hard-and-fast distinction between fact and fiction. While the West End audiences thrilled to its effervescent wit, the policeman's hand was just about to feel the playwright's collar; and when it did the show had to be taken off.

The Anglo-Irish Protestant Ascendancy into which Wilde was born was a displaced, deracinated group, at once internal exiles in Ireland and marginal to the British mainland. In fact, Wilde's career corresponds with uncanny exactness to the decline and fall of his own Anglo-Irish stock. The Church of Ireland to which they pledged allegiance was disestablished in his youth; popular disaffection with them gathered force throughout his lifetime; and his own disgrace and death around the turn of the nineteenth century coincided with the Land Acts which, in a remarkable revolution from above, dispossessed the Anglo-Irish gentry of their landed estates, which were distributed among their tenants. Like Jack Worthing in *Earnest*, then, Wilde's origin was also a terminus. He was born into a dying breed, and his own fractured identity reflected that of a people who could never say for certain who they were. Rather as the profligate Anglo-Irish were finally to pull the roof down on their own heads, so Wilde's reckless, spendthrift lifestyle seems to have been almost deliberately courting disaster. It was as though he were taunting the English Establishment to do its worst, and they were not slow to pick up the gauntlet. If he seems to have flirted with death, grappling the arrows of martyrdom to his body like his favourite saint Sebastian, it may be among other things because the aesthete in him was allured by death's luminous purity. In the end, his crime was to be too clever by half, to insist on the importance of not being earnest and to be too extravagantly, unabashedly himself.

Like many a literary émigré to British shores, Wilde set about the task of reinventing himself, becoming *plus anglais que les Anglais*, mimicking his hosts at the same time as he mocked them. It was never easy to say whether his imitation was flattery or parody, or whether the latter might be the sincerest form of the former. His epigrams are sagacious sayings gone suddenly awry, given a perverse twist or a suavely malicious sting in the tail. They take a conventional piece of English middle-class wisdom and dismantle it, turning it upside down or tearing it inside out, preserving its form while mischievously inverting its content. 'All bad poetry springs from genuine feeling', for example; or 'the only thing that one really knows about human nature is that it changes'. Wilde had the perversity of the colonial, who has only to spot a norm in order to feel the itch to violate it. His whole instinct was to improvise, experiment, make himself up as he went along. Among his many deviancies was his apparent ambition to become a major minor writer. If he made a point of being an 'original', it was partly because he was aware of how Ireland could seem like a poor parody or botched imitation of its metropolitan proprietors. It was this, among other things, which inspired him to outshine the natives at their own game, deploying their forms and conventions even more dexterously than they could themselves, and in doing so revealing something of their arbitrariness and absurdity. The very fact that such forms could be so easily borrowed implied that they were not as authentic as they appeared.

If Wilde was such a skilful mimic, it was partly because he was sceptical of the whole notion of a settled identity. It comes as no surprise that an offspring of the uncomfortably hyphenated Anglo-Irish should view all selfhood as provisional and problematic. The self for Wilde, as for his fellow countryman William Butler Yeats, was a mask, an enabling fiction, an ephemeral posture or theatrical performance. The nearest one could approach to truth was to cultivate a suitably ironic sense of one's own phoniness. A colonial people is less likely to be enthused by the idea of an unbroken continuity of selfhood than their rulers. There was little that was stable or continuous in the wretched history of Wilde's homeland. As an accomplished impersonator of himself, he had a profound faith in what Lenin once called the reality of appearances. Even the humbled, chastened self of *De Profundis* is at one level simply the latest of his dramatic personae. If he was seduced by the life of English high society, it was partly because he revelled in the unreality of its social forms and the paper-thinness of its personalities. In its mannered artifice, the world of Mayfair and Chelsea struck him as a work of art all in itself. If he was so fond of children, penning stories for them which are more politically explosive than they appear, it is partly because their innocence allowed him an escape from his own inveterate guilt, but also because children have as yet no very solid centre of self.

The Irish did not only have to ship cattle to the British; they also had to write much of their stage comedy for them.

From Goldsmith and Sheridan to Wilde, Shaw, Synge and Beckett, these English-speaking insider/outsiders were well placed to grasp English social and stage conventions; but as blow-ins from John Bull's other island, they could also cast a sardonic eye on their gratuitousness and ungroundedness, in ways less possible for home-grown writers. It is always easier for the outsider to spot something of the constructed nature of social reality, denaturalising what native thinkers tend to take spontaneously for granted. The tension between inside and outside viewpoints can then prove a fruitful source of comedy.

Wilde was one of a number of Irish writers who landed on the shores of Britain with little but their eloquence to hawk. What we remember of him in the end is talk, as one coruscating epigram tumbles on the heels of another in a kind of permanent haemorrhage of wit. From Burke and Sheridan to Edward Carson, Wilde's prosecuting counsel and former Dublin colleague, Britain was to profit from the rhetorical expertise of the Irish. Words cost nothing, and wit, fantasy and verbal exuberance were the edge these men could exert over a barren colonial existence. Those who hail from a colony which has witnessed the near destruction of its native language are likely to have a keener sensitivity to the word than those who can take their native speech casually for granted. Since the language they were writing in was not exactly their own, they tended to approach it with a finer self-consciousness than those lodged securely inside it, a self-consciousness that could then lend itself easily to modernist experiment. James Joyce remarked that the Irish were condemned to express themselves in a tongue not their own,[1] but for the same reason they could reinvent it with a brio and panache which English-born authors found hard to rival. To be marginal to a language and culture is also to be freer than the natives from its ruling forms and conventions, and thus to be less hamstrung by them. This is one of several reasons why, from Yeats to Beckett, Ireland proved more hospitable to modernism than any other region of the British Isles. Literary modernism is, among other things, the point at which language becomes newly aware of itself, a familiar enough situation to those already caught between two or more forms of speech. It is hard to imagine *Finnegans Wake* being written in Hampstead.

Nobody can live by culture alone, but Wilde came closer to doing so than almost any of his contemporaries. He is known as an exponent of art for art's sake, but this was not in his view a question of fleeing from life into art. On the contrary, it was a question of turning one's life into a work of art – of aestheticising one's everyday existence. To live aesthetically for Wilde meant not simply to strike an elegant pose or sport the right cut of waistcoat, but to realise one's creative powers in as full and free a way as possible. He was, in short, one of the last inheritors of the great Hellenic ideal of Romantic humanism. Art was a prototype of how to live, not a substitute for it. For Wilde, such self-realisation was not only compatible with morality; it *was* morality, in contrast to the leaden English moralism which, as Shaw wryly noted, the Irish had always found irresistibly amusing. A man who, like Wilde, found the death of Dickens's Little Nell uproariously funny was hardly afflicted by Arnoldian high-mindedness. By and large, Ireland is a notably non-moralistic society, a fact which may have to do with the minority status of its Protestant heritage. In this sense, it differs from the earnest, high-toned, hand-on-heart United States, whatever the historic ties between the two nations.

Wilde was his own finest work of art, a man who spent a lifetime sculpting himself into shape, a self-plagiarist and self-promoter with a religious devotion to his own self-fulfilment. This was partly because he was a shameless hedonist; but it was also because he recognised just how pathological the Victorian cult of selflessness and self-sacrifice could be. There could be something corrupt about English high-mindedness. Like William Blake, Wilde was aware of how altruism could serve as the sentimental face of egoism. He speaks in *The Soul of Man Under Socialism* of the 'sickly cant about duty' and the 'hideous cant about self-sacrifice',[2] conscious that the chief victims of this humbug were female. He had been the editor of a women's journal himself. Gwendolen in *The Importance of Being Earnest* maintains that the home is the proper sphere for a husband, and that once he begins to neglect his domestic duties he becomes painfully effeminate. Wilde despised the

Pharisaic brand of morality for which an action couldn't be virtuous unless it felt disagreeable. For this covertly sadistic ethic, the self was to be curbed rather than cultivated. In such a sanctimonious moral climate, Wilde's florid individualism was a politics in itself. In his resolve to make no bones about his own fulfilment, he brought down on his head the wrath and resentment of a social order that had grimly deferred its own gratification and was dismayed by the sight of one who refused to engage in this pointless self-punishment.

Wilde was well aware of how only a privileged cabal of individuals like himself could fashion themselves freely. Yet he also recognised how his own good fortune in this respect might prefigure a future in which the great majority of people might be able to do the same. In an outrageous paradox, his scandalous self-indulgence would yield a glimpse of utopia. The stereotypical feckless Mick who disliked excessive exertion would become both the idle English aristocrat and the socialist critic of sweated labour. This, in effect, is the theme of *The Soul of Man Under Socialism*, which looks forward to a time when labour will have been mechanised and men and women will consequently be set free for individual self-cultivation. The goal of socialism is individualism. If this is not quite how Marx himself would have put it, it is nonetheless close enough to his thought. Marx has a Romantic sense of the richness and diversity of individual lives, and holds that only under socialism can this spiritual wealth be emancipated.

He looks forward to what he calls 'the absolute working out of creative potentialities . . . [with] the development of all human powers as such the end in itself',[3] and writes in *Capital* that this 'blossoming forth' of human energies for their own sake requires the shortening of the working day.[4]

Socialism, in short, is about leisure, not labour. Whereas William Morris and the arts and crafts movement sought to convert work into a form of art, Marx and Wilde were intent on automating it so that men and women may have time for the more vital business of self-development, which can prove just as strenuous. In terms reminiscent of John Ruskin, with whom he worked while an undergraduate at Oxford, Wilde speaks of his 'regret that society should be constructed on such a basis that man has been forced into a groove in which he cannot freely develop what is wonderful, and fascinating, and delightful, in him – in which, in fact, he misses the true pleasure and joy in living'.[5] Under socialism, to be sure, labour will remain the basis of social existence; but material production will exist largely for the sake of culture, and culture (in the sense of free self-realisation) will achieve a certain precious autonomy from it. The more of an economic surplus one can generate, the more one can be emancipated from the necessity to toil. Like a successful course of psycho-therapy, then, the economic exists to do itself out of business. Marx and Wilde both believed in creating the material condi-tions in which we might be less slavishly dependent on the material. For us to be rid of our obsession with the economic, an economic revolution is essential. Only socialism can relieve us of this monomania, since under capitalism the drive to accumulation is endless. The logic of the marketplace ensures that we moderns work at least as hard as our Neolithic ancestors did. Technology is employed to intensify exploitation, not to abolish it. Wilde was conscious of how idly utopian his vision would appear to those whose ancestors had felt just the same about campaigns to end child labour or the slave trade. Any such radical change in the status quo, he pointed out, was bound to seem unreal to those whose sense of possibility was defined by it. A map of the world which did not include utopia, he remarked, was not even worth glancing at.

The Soul of Man Under Socialism argues that private property is inimical to true individualism, and must be done away with in the interests of the rich. It also claims that a good many of the poor are ungrateful, rebellious and disobedient, and are quite right to be so; that political agitators are a set of meddlers who sow the seeds of discontent, which is why they are so profoundly necessary; that altruism stands in the way of abolishing poverty; that social reform is short-sighted; that the family must be repudiated; and that historical progress comes about through revolt and agitation. It is hardly what the duchesses and Cabinet ministers who lionised the fashionable playwright wanted to hear. Perhaps, like Wilde himself from time to time, they were uncertain of how serious he was intending to be. The distinction between solemnity and frivolity is one of the many polarities he is out to dismantle.

Yet if *The Soul of Man* is the work of a socialist, it is also the product of a full-blooded elitist who despises the public and announces in most un-Herder-like fashion that 'the People bribe and brutalise'.[6] As usual, Wilde is indulging in two thinks at a time. Far from idealising the populace, he views them as bereft of both culture and civilisation, and admonishes the artist to ignore them. The distinction between elitism and socialism is in effect one between present and future. Wilde's logic here is brutal but precise. As long as men and women are calloused by poverty and drudgery, they can have no adequate response to culture, and art can only be compromised by seeking to accommodate their inept appreciation of it. It would therefore risk losing its true value, which is to provide the prototype of a future in which such poverty and drudgery would no longer exist. Where art was, there shall humanity be. Then, and then only, could those presently crushed by material circumstance flourish as free individuals. Ironically, then, the less art busies itself with current social problems, the more political it becomes. It is by remaining silent about such matters, repudiating realism and naturalism, that it can be of most help to humanity. For art to turn its face from social and political content is for it to highlight the autonomy of form; and since that autonomy is a question of free self-determination, it is a moral and political as well as aesthetic affair, foreshadowing the future kingdom of freedom within the realm of dire necessity.

Wilde's distinction between present and future is too absolute, as well as far too convenient for himself. It means that he can continue to indulge his taste for buying ruinously expensive furniture while viewing his actions as a foretaste of the socialist future. Even so, there is a steely realism about his vision of culture which is closer to Marx than it is to Schiller or Ruskin. Like Marx, he is concerned with the material conditions which would need to prevail for as many people as possible to become free spirits. It is because culture is generally grasped as the opposite of material matters that this question is so rarely posed. It is true that culture transcends material need, and to exceed strict necessity in this way, as *King Lear* recognises, is of our nature. Yet it is material conditions which determine how far this may be possible. Oscar Wilde may have been a dandy, and in *De Profundis* he sails perilously close to mistaking himself for Jesus Christ; yet there is an acuteness about his understanding of these issues which still has the capacity to surprise us, and not only because one does not expect such shrewdness from a bohemian layabout.

By the time of Wilde's death, the concept of culture had acquired a diversity of meanings. If it bulked large in the aesthetic movement to which he was drawn, it also played a key role in the revolutionary nationalism which he also found congenial. In the cult of art for art's sake, culture aspired to the status of a surrogate religion, yet it was also about to burst upon the world as a new form of mass production. It is to these various sources of the modern idea of culture that we can now turn.

CHAPTER FIVE

From Herder to Hollywood

THE MODERN CONCEPT of culture has many sources. The idea first came to prominence in the late eighteenth century as a critique of industrialism, but also as a rebuke to the notion of revolution. At about the same time, it became a key concept in the language of Romantic nationalism. As the nineteenth century unfolded, the notion of culture was caught up in debates about colonialism and anthropology, but also came to serve as a substitute for religious values that were on the wane. In the early decades of the twentieth century, culture burgeoned into a major industry, entering popular consciousness in unprecedented new ways. In the middle decades of the same century, it became a vital factor in new forms of political conflict, a phenomenon that has cropped up in our own time in the guise of multiculturalism and identity politics. We have already looked at the question of culture and revolution in the work of Edmund Burke, and can now say a word about these other issues.

In his *On the Aesthetic Education of Man* (1795), Friedrich
Schiller bemoans a condition in which:

everlastingly chained to a single little fragment of the
Whole, man himself develops into nothing but a fragment;
everlastingly in his ear the monotonous sound of the wheel
that he turns. He never develops the harmony of his being,
and instead of putting the stamp of humanity on his own
nature, he becomes nothing more than the imprint of his
occupation or of his specialised knowledge.[1]

Civilisation is at war with culture: the division of labour, an
increase in empirical knowledge, the complex machinery of
the modern state and a more rigorous distinction between
classes have all conspired to divide the inner nature of humanity,
so that 'a disastrous conflict sets its harmonious powers at vari-
ance'.[2] It is the lament of so-called *Kulturkritik*, one that will
echo down the modern age from William Blake to Herbert
Marcuse. Industrialism, technology, competitiveness, the
pursuit of profit and the division of labour have issued in
stunted capacities and dissociated powers. D.H. Lawrence
complains of 'the base forcing of all human energy into a
competition of mere acquisition'.[3] An inorganic society has
crippled our common humanity, while mechanistic modes of
thought have driven the creative imagination into exile. It is
the imagination that allows us to envisage alternative

possibilities to the present, a capacity which makes it a political force as well as an aesthetic one. Now, however, the visionary has yielded to the technocrat. Once upon a time, human nature formed a harmonious whole, as men and women realised their powers in all-round ways; today individuals are depleted and one-sided, mere fragments of humanity, functions of a mechanistic system rather than agents of their own history.

'In the very bosom of the most exquisitely developed social life', Schiller complains, 'egotism has founded its system.'[4] An industrial order powered by rivalry and acquisitiveness has sundered the traditional bonds between individuals, locking each of them into his or her own solitary space. The very fabric of society is consequently in peril. Human relationships have become contractual rather than organic. 'Our civilisation', Lawrence comments, 'has almost destroyed the natural flow of common sympathy between men and men, and men and women.'[5] Reason has been reduced to a bloodlessly instrumental mode of rationality, which does no more than calculate its own advantage. Nature has been drained of its inner vitality and reduced to so much dead matter for human manipulation. What holds sway over human lives is utility, for which nothing can be precious in itself. Things are worthwhile only in so far as they are means to achieve some end. Nothing is allowed to exist simply for the sake of it. Customs and affections which utility judges to be worthless are to be swept aside.

Sentiments and beliefs which threaten to distort an objective grasp of the world must be dispelled. With Schiller, Blake, Ruskin, Morris and Lawrence, we are speaking of the Romantic response to industrial capitalism – two phenomena that are twinned at birth; and it is in the name of culture, conceived of as a harmonious totality of human powers, that industrial society comes under judgement.[6]

This is a new development, though not one without precedent. For Jane Austen, for example, culture is essentially a matter of individual cultivation. It is a question of refinement and gentility. Yet since these values constitute a reproach to snobbery, self-interest, social climbing, mindless frivolity, moral crassness and material self-indulgence, they also have a bearing on the quality of social existence as a whole, as culture in the sense of the creative imagination does for Blake and Coleridge. For early eighteenth-century writers like Joseph Addison, Richard Steele and Anthony Ashley Cooper (third Earl of Shaftesbury), what others will later call 'culture' is known as 'politeness'; and politeness, as a form of graceful conduct which promotes social harmony, unites the moral and the aesthetic in much the same way that the idea of culture does for some later thinkers.

The impulse behind 'politeness', as later behind the idea of culture, was a political one. Post-Restoration England felt the need to construct a new public sphere that would act as a counterweight to church and court. Within this arena, some of the traditional aristocratic virtues (gentility, affability, elegance, refinement and the like) might be grafted on to an emergent urban middle class in sore need of a spot of polish. By this means, the two social classes would be welded together, and the governing power bloc thus consolidated. What one commentator describes as 'a new array of social, discursive and cultural institutions'[7] accordingly emerged in early eighteenth-century England, as clubs, coffee houses, assemblies, periodicals, gardens and theatres became new domains of enlightened middle-class discourse. Philosophy was to be emancipated from the study and cloister to play its part in a new project of moral and social self-fashioning. Reason was to be redefined as a question of conversation – of a free, equal, open dialogue between gentlemen over matters of ethics, taste, manners and good breeding. As Joseph Addison famously observed of his journal the *Spectator*, 'I have brought philosophy out of closets and libraries, schools and colleges, to dwell in clubs and assemblies, at tea-tables, and coffee-houses.'[8] Culture in the sense of certain cherished values was to be disseminated throughout culture in the sense of a shared form of life. It was an innovative, ambitious brand of cultural politics, and a remarkably effective one as well.

Authors like Friedrich Schiller inherit this social conception of culture in the face of new political pressures. Writing with the sound of French revolutionary terror in his ears, Schiller, like Burke, sees the need for a politics of consensus rather than one of brute coercion, and culture or the aesthetic provides a prototype of such harmony. His work *On the Aesthetic Education of Man* is among other things a political allegory, in which (as so often in the history of philosophy) the relations between reason and the senses are never far from the relations between ruling class and populace. It is as though the common people represent a mob of disorderly sensations which must be moulded into the shapeliness of a work of art, and culture is the process by which this redemptive project is to be achieved. If this fails to come about, Schiller warns, the state will be forced into the violent suppression of civil society, and will 'ruthlessly trample underfoot such powerfully seditious individualism in order not to fall a victim to it'.[9] The kid glove of culture conceals an iron political fist.

Behind the shift from culture as personal cultivation to culture as social salvation lies the arrival on the historical scene of an alarming new actor: the common people, and the industrial working class in particular. The labourer, observes Matthew Arnold, 'comes in immense numbers, and is rather raw and rough . . . And thus that profound sense of settled order and security, without which a society like ours cannot live or grow at all, sometimes seems to be beginning to threaten us with taking its departure.'[10] The urban masses are starting to shape history, but their middle-class masters know dismayingly little of their character and sentiments. A new inquiry must therefore be launched into darkest England, from the so-called industrial novel to the invention of sociology, the rhetoric of Thomas Carlyle to the researches of Friedrich Engels. What if history were no longer the work of great men but of vast, anonymous, subterranean social forces? And what then might become of the great men's culture? If nineteenth-century observers begin to speak nostalgically of the ancient Greeks, with their spiritual equipoise and supposedly organic society, it is not least because of factories and coal mines. Their fear is that if the masses prove incapable of cultivation, which is to say of behaving in a docile, self-disciplined way, then the very foundations of the state might be shaken. Unless culture becomes the way of life of Liverpool dockers as well as Oxford dons, culture, in the sense of the privileged existence of the latter, might well be doomed. One notes the assumption that culture, like reason, is an inherently bridling, tempering power. It was not seen to be in this light by the Futurists and Surrealists, however, any more than reason was regarded as a force for restraint by the Jacobins.

'Culture', writes Matthew Arnold, 'knows that the sweetness and light of the few must be imperfect until the raw and unkindled masses of humanity are touched with sweetness and light.'[11] The term 'culture' has discovered a new opposite, and its name is anarchy. The most celebrated cultural document of Victorian England, Arnold's *Culture and Anarchy* appeals to the idea of culture as a way of defusing popular disaffection. Culture is no longer a matter of unifying the rulers but of incorporating the ruled. By spreading sweetness and light, it will soothe savage plebeian breasts, dispel unruly passions, reconcile contending interests and bring concord to a fractured nation. We need, Arnold comments, 'to suppress the London roughs, but in behalf of the best self both of themselves and of all of us in the future'.[12] There are, in short, inferior races at home as well as abroad. Indeed, as the nineteenth century unfolded, the industrial working class came increasingly to be seen as a dark continent at the heart of Europe, a potentially mutinous power bred by civilisation but capable of sinking it without trace. The strife between colonialists and colonials was imported from the colonial margins to the metropolitan centre.

Another Victorian sage, John Ruskin, is rather more sympathetic than Arnold to the plight of the urban masses:

The great cry that rises from all our manufacturing cities, louder than their furnace blast, is all in very deed for this – that we manufacture everything there except men; we blanch cotton, and strengthen steel, and refine sugar, and shape pottery; but to brighten to strengthen, to refine or to form a living human spirit, never enters into our estimate of advantages.[13]

It is Schiller's argument applied to England's dark satanic mills. Culture – what Ruskin calls 'the felicitous fulfilment of function in living things'[14] – stands in severe judgement on civilisation:

> We have much studied and much perfected, of late, the great civilised invention of the division of labour; only we have given it a false name. It is not, truly speaking, the labour that is divided, but the men: – Divided into mere segments of men – broken into small fragments and crumbs of life . . . It is verily this degradation of the operative into a machine, which, more than any other evils of the times, is leading the mass of nations everywhere to vain, incoherent, destructive struggling for a freedom of which they cannot explain the nature to themselves.[15]

Once again, sympathy and self-interest are discreetly interwoven. If culture cannot restore a degree of wholeness to humanity, humanity might trample upon culture in its rage for justice. As with Arnold, the concept is deployed, quite explicitly, as a solvent of class warfare.

For this Romantic humanist tradition, culture in the sense of art is precious not only in itself, but because it offers an image of how culture in the sense of civilisation might be refurbished. As William Morris observes, 'it is the province of art to set the true ideal of a full and reasonable life before [humankind]'.[16] In similar spirit, Karl Marx finds his model of production not in coal mines or cotton mills but in the work of art. Communism means the free realisation of one's powers as ends in themselves, and art is a palpable image of this project. For both Morris and Marx, who represent that left wing of the Romantic humanist tradition, it offers an alternative to fruitless industrial toil. 'The aim of art', Morris remarks, 'is to destroy the curse of labour by making work the pleasurable satisfaction of our impulse towards energy.'[17] The goal of radical politics is to project one sense of culture into another – to extend a creative power currently confined to a minority to social existence as a whole.

There are problems, however, with the Romantic idea of self-realisation, as there are with any brand of ethics. Should one express *all* one's powers? What about one's capacity to maim and exploit? Perhaps one should foster only those capacities which are truly authentic – which spring straight from the core of the self. But how is one to judge which impulses are of this kind and which are not? In any case, what if my self-realisation clashes with yours? If the ideal is to realise one's capabilities in a balanced, well-rounded way, why should this be considered more valuable than a single unswerving commitment? Why shouldn't someone whose life is devoted to the pursuit of justice live as abundantly as someone who can abseil, whistle entire symphonies, speak Estonian and grasp the principles of set theory? Diversity, once more, does not always trump singularity.

The Romantic concept of self-realisation tends to assume that the self's faculties are inherently positive. The only problem is that they are being blocked by some external obstacle: the state, law, despotism, patriarchy, superego, imperial authority, the governing class, bourgeois morality and so on. But what if the impediments to freedom lie closer to home than that? In Freud's view, we internalise the Law in the form of the superego, which means that to violate its diktats is to risk doing injury to ourselves. Burke, too, is aware that the only effective sovereignty is one which we make our own. It is this that Antonio Gramsci was later to call a hegemonic power, as opposed to a coercive one. For Freud, we are also inveterate masochists who love the very Law in whose presence we tremble, which further complicates the matter. Power and desire are not simply antagonists but co-conspirators. In any case, how can we know what we desire until we give expression to it? Even then, it is not obvious that we always know what we want. Since we are not transparent to ourselves, as the Romantic libertarian tends to assume, we can easily be deceived over the question. There are false desires and specious forms of freedom. Besides, what if, as Freud suspects, we harbour an unconscious wish not to fulfil our desires, since to realise them would be to abolish them? What if desire is out to defer its own gratification? In Freud's view, there is a flaw or glitch at the heart of desire which deflects its aim and turns it awry. There is also always a residue of it left unrealised, however fully and freely we express ourselves. Discontent is of our nature, and the science of discontent is known as psychoanalysis.

Not much of this is taken on board by the Romantic humanist tradition, a lineage which includes Karl Marx. Marx would seem to assume that human powers and capacities are positive in themselves, and that we can have fairly direct access to their nature. Human beings may be mystified and manipulated, but they are not constitutively self-opaque. In this view, there would appear nothing botched or intractable at the heart of humanity, whereas Freud sketches his own version of original sin. Even so, Marx turns the Romantic vision in a new direction. What he does is harness it to an actual political force: the labour and socialist movements. It is a move that William Morris will repeat in the English *fin-de-siècle*. Without such a material incarnation, the idea of culture is bound to remain abstract and academicist. Unlike Schiller and Arnold, both Marx and Morris inquire into the question of what material conditions would be necessary for social life to prove more fulfilling, and find an answer to their query in the abolition of capitalism. In particular, Marx offers a response to the question of how my self-realisation is to avoid colliding with yours. His implicit recommendation would appear to be: realise the self only in a way which provides the means for others freely to do the same. It is this that he has in mind when he remarks in *The Communist Manifesto* that, in communist society, the free development of each will be the condition for the free development of all. It is not a knockdown solution to the problem; nor is it original to Marx himself. Like much else, he lifted it from Hegel. But it is a richly suggestive ethics all the same.

Without the move that Marx and Morris make, the concept of culture remains a resourceful critique of modern civilisation, but a politically ineffectual one. Culture becomes a refuge from civil society rather than a means of transforming it. From Coleridge to F.R. Leavis, it sets itself above the inferior domain of politics, work and citizenship. It is a moral, personal or spiritual affair, aloof for the most part from the material realm of famines and economic slumps, genocide and women's oppression. Like religion, it provides some spiritual compensation for what it tends to castigate as an almost wholly sterile civilisation. Indeed, there are times at which, from its Olympian height, it can see hardly anything affirmative in a degenerate modern existence. The link between culture and politics that Burke considered so vital, is gradually eroded.

* * *

While the notion of culture was becoming a critique of industrialism around the turn of the eighteenth century, it was also laying the foundations of Romantic nationalism. Herder, as we have seen already, was one of its most impassioned advocates. The idea of the autonomous, self-determining nation is not much more than a couple of centuries old, even though nations themselves are fond of fantasising that their origins lie buried deep in the mists of time. Nationalism was to prove the most successful revolutionary movement of the modern era, dismantling empires, toppling tyrants and bringing a host of new political states to birth. Yet it was to some extent, in the words of one commentator, 'the invention of literary men',[18] which is not usually the case with world-transformative projects; and the chief reason for this was the prominence it assigned to the idea of culture. As a British army officer remarked when his men executed the nationalist rebels of Dublin in 1916: 'We have done Ireland a service: we have rid it of some second-rate poets.' It was through revolutionary nationalism above all that the concept of culture, however abstract and ethereal it might seem at first sight, did indeed succeed in refashioning the face of the earth. The desire of nations to be free of their colonial masters was to prove the most potent coupling of culture and politics of the modern age, far more effective than the so-called cultural politics of our own period.

Unlike civic nationalism, which concerns itself with such questions as citizenship and political rights, Romantic nationalism is a spiritual principle before it is a political programme. It is a poetic brand of politics, hospitable to image, archetype and the creative imagination, as much concerned with myth, symbolism and blood sacrifice as with protecting indigenous industries or thinking up a name for one's currency. Only when colonial nations finally achieve their independence does the poetry of revolt yield to the prose of constructing a state and building an economy. One author describes Romantic nationalism as the elevation of sentiment from the private to the political realm.[19] At an extreme, it can figure as a secular version of religion, one of the more successful of modernity's numerous surrogates for the Almighty. Like God, the nation is sacred, indivisible, self-sustaining, without origin or end, the ground of all being, the source of identity, transcendent of the individual and a cause worth dying for. There is a galaxy of nationalist heroes, as there is a pantheon of saints and martyrs. Like religion, nationalism couples everyday life with visionary idealism. The nation, observed Herder's colleague Johann Gottlieb Fichte, is a work of God.

With the rise of national liberation movements, poets, artists and scholars attain a public prominence to which they are hardly accustomed in less turbulent times. Intellectuals can now become social activists in the manner of a Yeats or a Léopold Senghor, placing their work at the service of their country and proclaiming their solidarity with the more menial members of the nation. Historians, philologists and antiquarians find themselves dragged from their studies and thrust into the political limelight. Shelley saw poets as the unacknowledged legislators of humankind, a description that W.H. Auden thought more appropriate to the secret police; but with the rise of anti-colonial wars, a number of nationalist artists became legislators in reality. Nationalist movements tend to give rise to a body of distinguished artistic culture, and thus forge a link between culture as the arts and culture as a way of life. It would be hard to say the same of neo-liberalism or social democracy.

Romantic nationalists like Herder view nations as unified, self-creating and self-determining. In this sense, they can be seen to resemble works of art. It would be hard to overrate the havoc this doctrine has wreaked in the modern world. For one thing, there are no unified nations. Most societies are ethnically diverse, and all of them are socially divided. Nations are political constructs, not natural phenomena. If the citizens of a region or country are suppressed by a foreign power, they have a right to self-determination; but it is arguable that they possess such a right because they are people, not because they are *a* people. It is Romantic mysticism to believe that being Swiss or Somali automatically entitles you to your own government. What is wrong with oppressing Angolans is not the fact that there is something inherently precious about being Angolan but that there is something inherently offensive about being oppressed. Individual Angolans may well be inherently valuable, but that is a different matter. A group of people of British origin who have long inhabited another country do not have a right to establish their sovereignty there simply because they are British. This is how Northern Ireland, along with its subsequent history of bloodshed, arrived on the agenda. There is no natural connection between having an ethnic identity and exercising political citizenship. Being colonised by others is objectionable on much the same grounds that being thrown out of your own home by bullying neighbours is. As far as the injustice of it goes, the fact that those who dispossess you spring from another race or nation is neither here nor there.[20] Colonialism is at root a political and economic reality, not (as some postcolonial theory imagines) a cultural one. A benevolent brand of colonialism like Edmund Burke's may seek to cherish and protect a native culture, but this is no reason why it should not be resisted.

We have seen that for Burke culture could be both a way of imposing power and a mode of contesting it. Much the same ambiguity can be found in nationalism. If it was the creed of the Nazis, it was also the means by which colonial peoples could shake off their overlords and achieve a degree of self-determination. Nationalism is both the British Empire and the global revolt against it. Anti-colonialism is both America's uprising against the British and the mutiny of one down-at-heel nation after another against the dominion of the United States. It would be hard to find a more self-contradictory form of politics.

If culture is what allows us to survive and flourish, it is also what men and women are prepared to kill for, a fact to which both anti-colonial insurrections and subsequent ethnic conflicts bear witness. Only seriously weird people are prepared to kill for Balzac or Berlioz, but large numbers of men and women will slaughter, or be martyred, for culture in the sense of an ethnic, religious or national identity. Language, belief, kinship, symbol, heritage and homeland are now potentially lethal sources of dissension. They are zones of contention rather than nodes of unity. This marks a seismic shift in the history of cultural ideas. For thinkers like Schiller, Coleridge and Arnold, culture is above all a force for reconciliation. It allows us to transcend our sectarian squabbles, converging instead on the ground of our common humanity. If literature and the arts are indispensable, it is not least because they seem to encapsulate that humanity in peculiarly graphic, sensuously immediate form, in a way that nothing as anaemic as philosophy or political science can rival. They are the means by which we can almost literally weigh in our palms the fundamental values by which we are supposed to live.

Moved by the harmonising power of culture, we are able to rise above our petty material preoccupations with rank, class, power, gender, ethnicity, social inequality and so on, suspending these disputes in a higher sphere. If there seems no ready political solution to such antagonisms, culture will furnish us with a spiritual one. It thus performs a function similar to that of religion, which is one reason why it has so often aspired to become a secular version of such belief. Like religious faith in Marx's renowned phrase, culture (or the humanities) is the heart of a heartless world and the soul of soulless conditions. It is also often enough the opium of the intelligentsia. As such, it is at once invaluable and largely ineffectual. If it can be a solvent of human strife, it is only by providing an imaginary resolution of such antagonisms, one which might then distract our attention from the need for real-life ones. There is cultural as well as theological pie in the sky. If culture in this sense of the word can foster values which have been driven from the public realm as superfluous and dysfunctional, it is not least because it stands at a disabling distance from that workaday world, and so is ill-equipped to transform it. The problem for authors like Schiller, Arnold and Ruskin is that, with the rise of industrial capitalism, the need for such a transformation has now become pressing, but the means of its achievement are as murky as ever.

What happens with the rise of revolutionary nationalism, however, is that culture ceases to be part of the solution and instead becomes part of the problem. It is no longer the sworn enemy of politics; rather, it is the very idiom in which political demands are framed, articulated and fought out. It descends from heaven to earth, still trailing clouds of glory, to become an active political force. If this is true of nationalism, it is equally true of the so-called identity politics – feminism, ethnic struggles, gay rights and so on – which follows hard on its heels. At the same time as the capitalist labour market goes truly global, men and women migrate across the planet in search of work, converting what were once largely mono-ethnic nations into multicultural ones. In this way, too, culture is redefined as part of the problem, as tensions between different ethnic groups pose a threat to political stability. In the form of ethnicity and immigration, though not in the form of Stendhal and Schumann, culture is now a daily subject of debate in the Western heartlands. The idea that human cultures can overlap, or that one might share in a range of them simultaneously, is by no means new. There are countless examples of such hybrid life-forms throughout history. What is new is the fact that a high degree of cultural diversity will be the routine condition of social existence from now on. An ideal of unity and purity can usually be found lurking beneath the classical notion of culture, which has now for the most part been put to rest. Culture and purity no longer march hand in hand.

'The milieu in which the modern anthropological notion of culture was born', writes Robert J.C. Young, 'was class and race conflict.'[21] Given the unholy alliance between colonial power and nineteenth-century anthropology, the concept of culture is contaminated to its core by racist ideology. In fact, one of the sources of the word 'culture' is the Latin verb *colere*, meaning to occupy or inhabit. A word that stands for some of the most exalted of human achievements also smacks of some of the most unspeakable. It is hard for us today to rid the concept of its role in the 'scientific' study of premodern peoples, one that tended to freeze them in their subhuman otherness.

At the very moment that they suppressed colonial peoples, however, the colonialists also exoticised them. In the case of Ireland, as Luke Gibbons writes:

The Celt was granted an unlimited poetic licence as a consolation for the loss of political power, in keeping with the elegiac note in Romanticism where communities excluded from the march of progress – Orientals, Africans, native Americans, or, closer to home, an idealised peasantry – enjoyed an afterlife in the realms of the imagination.[22]

Values which a utilitarian civilisation has expelled as so much surplus baggage – sensuality, bodily grace, sexual energy, imaginative brio – take up an imaginary home on the colonial margins, as they do on the artistic ones. They can then be consumed at a judicious distance. Roughly speaking, the colonialists have civilisation, while their colonial subjects have culture. We envy those subjects because they are guileless and sensual, whereas they envy us for our dishwashers and cathedrals. They are more organic than us, while we are more stylish than they are. If there is one piece of culture sufficient to discredit this banal wisdom, it is art, since art can boast no evolutionary progress. Aboriginal art is as sophisticated as abstract Expressionism. There is no upward trek from the Icelandic sagas to Saul Bellow.

As the colonialists pursue their civilising mission, they encounter a striking diversity of cultures, most of them (at least until they themselves arrive on the scene) in tolerably good working order; and this is bound to prove somewhat disquieting, not least when the business of foisting your sovereignty on such cultures may require a robust faith in your own racial or cultural supremacy. 'May', because subjugating others does not necessarily involve a belief in one's own pre-eminence; but even when it does not, the sheer proliferation of other life-forms may be enough to rattle your faith in your own. That there are innumerable different ways of doing things, most of them reasonably viable, is not exactly what you want to hear, not least when you are busy sending your gunboats up foreign rivers. It smacks too much of a cultural relativism that risks corroding your self-assurance, as with the colonialist-turned-nihilist Kurtz of Joseph Conrad's *Heart of Darkness*. Kurtz starts out as a bearer of civilised sweetness and light to colonial Africa; but because this encounter with an alien culture serves to highlight the contingent nature of his own concept of civility, his faith in the white man's burden soon turns to ashes in his mouth.

There is a parallel to this situation in E.M. Forster's *A Passage to India*, a novel in which the middle-class Englishwoman Mrs Moore finds her identity grievously undermined by an encounter with cultural difference in colonial India. As a result, she keels over into a nihilistic disgust with humanity and loses her grip on life. There is a sense in which she dies of cultural relativism, a privileged kind of demise. If Kurtz shifts from enlightened colonialist to barbarous nihilist, Mrs Moore is a Bloomsbury liberal whose pluralism has been pressed too far. The fact that she is a liberal rather than (like her imperialist prig of a son) a stiff-necked chauvinist, a woman with an instinctive respect for the customs of others, fails to save her from this ontological collapse, which suggests just how deep the problem runs. In fact, it is her sensitivity which brings her to such spiritual fatigue.

The novel, however, is careful to relativise her collapse into relativism. It is not to be taken as the final truth. Perhaps one would be less susceptible to such disorientation if one had a suitably ironic sense of the fragility of one's own values in the first place. Mrs Moore has come to recognise the difficulties of cross-cultural communication and the intractable nature of human misunderstanding, along with the fact that no particular set of cultural values is underwritten by the universe itself; but it does not follow from this that such values are vacuous. From the novel's own standpoint, her despair is premature. All the same, there is always the possibility of a cultural perspective that can sabotage one's own. Perhaps there is a well-nigh infinite regress of them. Gulliver speculates in Swift's novel that there might be a people somewhere in the world to whom the giant Brobdingnagians would look like tiny Lilliputians. Cultural relativism was by no means unknown to the eighteenth century.

Indigenous peoples cannot be entirely different from oneself, since there would then be no possibility of holding them down. It is hard to impose your authority on men and women who do not understand that rifles can kill. Yet they must not resemble you too closely either, since then they are likely to appear as a monstrous parody of yourself, estranging your own conduct to the point where you are forced to view it in an unpleasantly new light. Gulliver cannot dismiss the Lilliputians as mere freaks or exotics since their behaviour is too unnervingly close to the least admirable features of his own compatriots. The book encourages us to expect that these minuscule creatures will be alien to ourselves, only to pull the rug out from under the reader by showing that they are intimates in all the most disconcerting ways. Greed, vanity and a lust for power, so the suggestion goes, are universal characteristics. If Europeans complacently believe that their own nature is universal, Swift turns this faith satirically back upon them.

Swift was a member of the Anglo-Irish Protestant Ascendancy, the social class in Ireland lambasted by Edmund Burke, and as both English and Irish could never be sure whether he was conqueror or victim, installed at the heart of power or banished to its periphery. He is both thoroughly bound up with Ireland and looking in from the outside. The boneheaded Gulliver displays a similar ambiguity. He is either too remote from the cultures he encounters, or too pathetically eager to conform to them (a gull, in short). He is foolishly proud of the meaningless title the Lilliputians bestow on him, and hotly denies having sex with a microscopic Lilliputian female despite the comic impossibility of such congress. When he is presented to the king of Brobdingnag, however, he turns out to be too narrowly imprisoned within his own cultural norms, boasting of his nation's military might with a chuckleheaded chauvinism the king finds detestable. The natives of Brobdingnag reflect on how contempt-ible their own character must be if it can be mirrored in such a despicable insect as Gulliver himself. The whole text of *Gulliver's Travels* turns on this interplay between the intimate and the outlandish. The familiar is made strange, while what appears at first sight to be foreign turns out often enough to be too close for comfort.

Gulliver is eager to distinguish himself from the repulsive, shit-coated Yahoos, while being aware that the governing breed of Houyhnhnms regards him as no better than a Yahoo himself. He is caught between the two species rather as Swift himself is caught between the English governors and the Gaelic masses. There are those 'upper' natives in the colonies (the Anglo-Irish, for example) who dissociate themselves from the common people and identify with the colonialists, as Gulliver throws in his lot with the Houyhnhnms; but the colonialists themselves will never embrace these displaced souls as equals, and the people will spurn them as well. Like Gulliver, then, one will end up with the worst of both worlds, lacking both the superior culture of the Houyhnhnm rulers and the rude natural vigour of their Yahoo underlings.

The situation, in short, is more complex and contentious than a simple 'colonials versus colonialists' distinction would suggest. There are those colonial citizens, for example, who reject both the native culture and the lifestyle of the colonial-ists – who demand political autonomy, but doubt that the best way to achieve it is through a Herder-like revival of the nation's imperilled language and culture. In the Irish context, the nationalist leaders Daniel O'Connell and Charles Stewart Parnell were both of this persuasion. In their view, colonisation was a political indignity, but one which brought with it the means by which the nation could spring from backwardness to modernity. Yet there were also groups like the Young Irelanders who held that this would simply lead the country to become a poor imitation of its colonial masters. Instead, Ireland had to find its own distinctive cultural path to political autonomy, a view also popular among the Gaelic Revivalists. If some of these intellectuals idealised the culture of the folk, so did some of the folk.

There are likely to be renegades among the colonial ruling class who embrace the culture of the people even more fervently than the people do themselves. In Ireland, Yeats, J.M. Synge and Lady Gregory may serve as examples. As members of an Anglo-Irish coterie, they are uncomfortably conscious of themselves as a second-class ruling caste in the country, patronised or sidelined by the politicians at Westminster, and as such they feel some spontaneous sympathy for their rather more grievously dispossessed fellow country people, to whom they themselves form a rather more privileged parallel. Others, like Swift, may champion the common people while lacking any genuine fellow-feeling for them. It would not be too much to claim that Swift detested the Gaelic poor on whose behalf he spoke out so eloquently. Some citizens will be complicit with the colonial government; others, like Swift, will be semi-complicit, while some nationalists will resent colonial rule because they are keen to form a political elite themselves, and find their path to this goal blocked by foreign occupation.

For a governing class to hold down a nation abroad may also serve to buttress its power at home. At least the humblest of its native citizens now have someone to feel superior to, and so may feel less aggrieved about their own lowly status. Marx thought this was true of British working-class attitudes to Irish immigrants. On the other hand, the working class at home may strike up a degree of political solidarity with colonial rebels abroad, which is rather less to their masters' taste. There are also likely to be those among the metropolitan elite who feel some sympathy for such rebels, as we have seen in the case of Members of Parliament like Burke and Sheridan. Others, again like Burke, may condemn the colonial rulers because they fear that their high-handed behaviour is driving the native population into disaffection, thus putting the whole colonial project in jeopardy. For their part, the common people tend be inconsistent in their view of their foreign overlords, veering between deference and defiance. In Ireland, members of the rural tenantry might read a loyal address to their landlord in the morning only to creep out to hamstring his cattle at night. Wearied by these contradictions, there will also be those who shake the dust of the colony disdainfully off their heels, like James Joyce and Samuel Beckett.

One of the lessons of Swift's novel is that one must have a suitably ironic sense of the relativity of one's own culture, but not to the point where, like Gulliver, who ends up trotting around neighing like a horse, one repudiates it altogether and falls into madness and despair. You must try to grasp your own situation from the outside in the name of true judgement, but not thereby topple headlong into scepticism and self-loathing. There is no absolute vantage-point outside culture, but this is not to say that we are doomed to be the helpless prisoners of any particular cultural set-up. The anthropologist Claude Lévi-Strauss writes in his *Tristes Tropiques* that to feel one's way into other cultures is to grasp one's own form of life more fully, since what we find in the behaviour of others is an arrestingly unfamiliar version of the laws which regulate our own symbolic universe. For these laws to be made strange is for us to look upon them with fresh insight. Yet it is only because we share some common ground with others that such self-estrangement is possible. If there were merely difference, there could be no such transformative dialogue. In encountering another culture, then, we are also brought to confront a certain ineradicable otherness in ourselves, gazing with new eyes on our own activities through a recognition of these others as our kinsfolk. We must see ourselves, Lévi-Strauss remarks in his *Structural Anthropology*, 'as an other among others'.

* * *

Another source of the modern idea of culture is the death of God. Perhaps culture can fill the God-shaped hole scooped out by secular modernity. Since I have written on this subject at length elsewhere, I shall not rehearse it in any detail here.[23] Suffice it to say that the modern era is littered with failed substitutes for God, from reason, spirit, art, science and the state to the people, the nation, humanity, society, the unconscious and Michael Jackson. Among these botched surrogates for the Almighty, the idea of culture looms up as one of the most plausible. In fact, there is an etymological relation between the word 'culture' and the religious term 'cult'. A great many aesthetic terms (symbol, creation, inspiration, revelation, unity, epiphany, autonomy and so on) are bits of displaced theology. Like religion, culture brings the most cherished of values to bear on everyday activity. Like religion, too, it is a question of fundamental truths, spiritual depths, right conduct, imperishable principles and a communal form of life. It also has its rituals, high priests, revered icons and places of worship.

Matthew Arnold regards culture as absolute and transcendent, while one of the most influential of twentieth-century literary critics, F.R. Leavis, treats literature in effect as a substitute religion. His fellow critic I.A. Richards declared that poetry 'is capable of saving us'.[24] For a while, then, there seemed good reason to trust that culture might step into God's shoes, in an age in which his apparent disappearance threatened to become a source of social instability. Social order, so it was considered, depends on morality, and morality has traditionally depended in turn on religious faith; so how are the foundations of the state to survive the demise of the Deity? Religion is the most powerful, persistent, universal, tenacious, deep-seated form of popular culture that history has ever witnessed, one which offers to bridge the gulf between mass and minority, laity and priesthood, everyday behaviour and absolute truth, culture as spiritual and culture as anthropological; and if its hold over humanity has begun to loosen, then the values it holds dear must migrate elsewhere. For all its promise, however, culture proved unable to take over the baton from the Supreme Being. In the minority, aesthetic sense of the term, it involved too tiny a fraction of society, in contrast to the billions of men and women whom religion has been able to inspire; while in its broader anthropological sense it was too riven by conflict to provide a source of unity, uplift and consolation. If culture as the arts was too esoteric to do service for grace and redemption, culture as everyday life was both too humdrum and too contentious to do so.

As the Victorian sages brooded upon these questions, what was waiting in the wings was a dramatic transformation of the whole nature of culture – one in which culture in the artistic sense was indeed to become a majority activity, but not at all in the sense that William Morris had hoped. Culture had long since been bound up with commerce and technology, but now, with the advent of film, radio, television, recorded music, advertising, the popular press and popular fiction, it was rapidly becoming a major industry in its own right. From the early twentieth century onward, the mass production of fantasy was to prove a lucrative trade, as the so-called culture industry was born.

In what one commentator has called the greatest change ever in the history of cultural production,[25] culture was now for the most part no longer a critique of modern manufacture but a highly profitable sector of it. It belonged to the material infrastructure of capitalism quite as much as the refining of sugar or the harvesting of wheat. Popular culture had surged to the fore, just as Herder had dreamed; but for the most part it was a culture consumed by the masses, not one produced by them. Mass culture might provide some relief from labour, yet it also transferred to the sphere of entertainment the very mechanised processes which characterised the world of industrial production.

A more dissident minority culture continued to flourish, but it had been forced onto the back foot, taking shelter in the artistic coterie, the little magazine, the small press or the cosmopolitan café. If popular culture was being commodified, the 'high' work of art sought to avoid this indignity by turning its back on everyday existence, thickening its language, dislocating its meanings, garbling its narratives and fragmenting its forms in order to avoid the humiliation of being too easily consumed. Rather than allow itself to be reduced to a cog in the system of mass production, it insisted on its own purity and autonomy. The work of art had nothing as vulgar as a social purpose. Unlike the commodity, it existed as a value in itself. The artistic experiment we know as modernism has many sources, but a strenuous resistance to mass culture is certainly one of them. Indeed, the two phenomena were born at the same historical moment. For all their mutual antagonism, however, they could both be accused of breeding socially convenient illusions. With its fake immediacy and fantasy solutions, a good deal of mass culture offered its consumers a form of false utopia; but so, too, did some high art, which may not have provided reconciliation in its disenchanted content, but which often enough sought to do so in its unifying forms.

Marxism has traditionally drawn a distinction between what it calls the 'base' of society, which includes property relations and productive activity in particular, and the 'superstructure', which ranges from law and art to politics and ideas. The media, as socio-economic set-ups devoted to manufacturing forms of consciousness, reveal a peculiarly close relation between these two realms. If they are 'objective' phenomena, they also give rise to 'subjective' modes of experience. To some extent, to be sure, this is true of all cultural forms. Imagine a novel which is ambitious in scope, crammed with complex events, full of intricate narrative twists and populated by a broad array of characters. Such a work can exist only because of print technology. Its very artistic form is shaped by this material fact. Nobody could copy out such a lengthy text many times over by hand, as an Elizabethan poet might pass a handful of copies of his love lyrics around a circle of fellow-courtiers.

In today's media, however, this relation between artistic forms and material facts is more palpable than ever. Think, for example, of the average US television news programme, if one may dignify such stuff with the title of an artistic form. The fact that the newscasters are selected among other things for being easy on the eye, as well as for the resonant pitch of their voices, the faux-genial banter between them, the abrupt leaping from one news item to another, the sensationalised presentation, the monosyllabic scripts, the fact that camera shots in film footage are rarely sustained for more than a few seconds, the absence of in-depth analysis so as not to bore less sophisticated viewers, the relentless focus on home-grown news even if a nuclear war has just broken out in Yorkshire – all this bespeaks the overriding imperative of securing the largest possible audience for the sake of the greatest possible profit. The experiential is shaped by the economic at almost every point. It is the advertising breaks that ultimately dictate that the syntax of such news programmes should be simple, vocabulary basic, tones histrionic, teeth sparkling and searching interviews with Noam Chomsky non-existent.

Culture, so the complaint used to run, was too aloof from the rest of social life. Now, however, with the evolution of the culture industry, it permeates that existence from end to end. If it was once too remote from the everyday to provide a convincing critique of it, it is now too bound up with it to do so. There were times when 'high' culture was able to turn its distance from everyday life to political advantage. Free of any definitive social function, it could gesture in utopian style to an alternative form of social existence. We have seen an example of this in the work of Oscar Wilde. By and large, this utopian function of art proved to be a casualty of culture's integration into general commodity production. Even so, when it comes to popular culture, one is speaking of enrichment as well as impoverishment. We have noted already that the distinction between high and popular culture cannot be mapped on to one between precious and worthless. There is a good deal in mass culture (Hitchcock, Planxty, John Coltrane, Philip K. Dick, Ian Rankin, Morrissey, Monty Python) that is of superlative quality, and quite a chunk of 'high' culture (Emerson, Matthew Arnold, the later Browning, Conrad's *Heart of Darkness*, the fiction of Alice Munro) that is considerably overrated. Besides, 'high' culture can itself be transformed by its popular counterpart. For the first time in history, it has become possible for millions of people to listen simultaneously to a Verdi opera or watch a Chekhov play. A film or television production of a Dickens or Jane Austen novel can bear fruit in hundreds of thousands of bookshop sales.

This, however, would be scant comfort to such custodians of high culture as F.R. Leavis, who writes in his *Mass Civilisation and Minority Culture* that:

> in any period it is upon a very small minority that the discerning appreciation of art and literature depends . . . Upon this minority depends our power of profiting by the finest human experience of the past; they keep alive the subtlest and most perishable parts of tradition. In their keeping . . . is the language, the changing idiom, upon which fine living depends, and without which distinction of spirit is thwarted and incoherent. By 'culture' I mean the uses of such a language.[26]

Unlike John Ruskin and William Morris, Leavis does not imagine that the idea of culture might point to a different form of civilisation. Instead, its task is to fight a rearguard action against the 'lazy and unintelligent' masses, as Freud called them in *The Future of an Illusion*. Yet what, inquires Raymond Williams, do we mean by 'mass' here?

> Do we mean a democracy dependent on universal suffrage, or a culture dependent on universal education, or a reading public dependent on universal literacy? If we

find the products of mass civilisation so repugnant, are we to identify the suffrage or the education or the literacy as the agent of decay?[27]

None of them, is Williams's own reply. They are all to be ranked among the precious achievements of modern civilisation, in which the high-toned critics of modernity can see nothing but cultural tawdriness. Such critics also refuse for the most part to investigate the root-causes of this pervasive cheapening of experience, much of which, as Williams himself points out, springs from the profit motive. In their view, there can be no solution to these ills in a present degraded beyond repair. Instead, Leavis looks back nostalgically to the so-called organic society of pre-industrial England. Williams, by contrast, is concerned to remind us of 'the penury, the petty tyranny, the disease and mortality, the ignorance and frustrated intelligence that were also among its ingredients'.[28]

Mass culture evolved in two stages. First, it extended its influence into almost every crevice of society; then it began to merge with the rest of social existence, so that the distinction between culture and society grew increasingly uncertain. Politics became increasingly a matter of image, icon, style and spectacle. Commerce and production relied more and more on packaging, design, branding, advertising and public relations. Personal relationships were mediated by technological texts and images. The era of postmodernism had set in.

For a number of reasons, then, culture has shed its innocence. Indeed, the history of the modern age is among other
things the tale of the gradual demystification of this noble
ideal. From its sublime status in the thought of thinkers like
Schiller, Herder and Arnold, it becomes caught up in a danger-
ously rhapsodic brand of nationalism, entangled in racist
anthropology, absorbed into general commodity production
and embroiled in political conflict. Far from providing an
antidote to power, it turns out to be deeply collusive with it.
Rather than being what might save us, it might need to be put
firmly back in its place, as we shall now go on to argue.

The Hubris of Culture

UNLIKE MEDIA MOGULS, literary critics have always harboured doubts about their own importance. On the one hand, there is no denying that literature deals with the most fundamental of human realities, which may be enough to confer a degree of status on those who trade in it. On the other hand, ever since it deserted the public sphere to enter academia, the study of literary works has been a peripheral pursuit, to the point where it is not hard to imagine university departments of literature (indeed of the arts and humanities in general) becoming a thing of the past. Academic literary studies were greeted with cries of genteel derision when they first emerged (did a gentleman really require formal instruction in the literary arts of his own language, any more than in the art of how to carry his rifle while out on a shoot?), and must nowadays confront a more streetwise form of scepticism (do such recondite pursuits really contribute anything to a buoyant economy?).

It was the concept of popular culture, among other new developments, that rode to the rescue of a literary criticism at risk of losing its social relevance altogether. Once literary scholars ventured into the study of film, media and popular fiction, there could be no doubt that they had some plausible claim to centrality. They were, after all, engaged with artefacts consumed by millions of ordinary people. We have seen already that a different kind of centrality was assigned to those literary intellectuals who threw in their lot with revolutionary nationalism – men and women who, in exchanging the seminar room for the battlefield, could now lay claim to world-historical status. The Irish revolutionary Thomas MacDonagh, having conducted his last university class (on Jane Austen) in Dublin, left the campus to take part in the anti-colonial insurrection of Easter 1916, and later met his death at the hands of the British army. The road from *Mansfield Park* to militant patriot proved shorter than one might imagine. Once the revolutionary nationalist tide began to ebb, it was ethnic politics and postcolonial issues which helped to secure a broader role for cultural theory, just as the growth of the culture industry had done already. The so-called war on terror played its part, too, as cultural affinities, ethnic identities and religious convictions billowed into global political discord. Before then, however, cultural and literary studies had been lent a powerful new lease of life by the rise of sexual politics, which for the past few decades has been one of its major preoccupations. By the beginning of the twenty-first century, then, there seemed no doubt that the concept of culture had a future which would last at least as long as *jihad*, and which only the demise of cinema and television, along with the disappearance of libido from the face of the earth, might seriously imperil. Culture as a concept had not only come of age, but seemed in some quarters to reign supreme.

It was, however, in danger of overrating its own importance. Take, for example, the ambiguity of the term 'culture industry'. If the word 'industry' is a measure of how far cultural production has extended its reach throughout modern civilisation, it is also a reminder that the chief motives for this are by no means cultural ones. Like General Motors, Hollywood and the media exist primarily for the sake of their shareholders. It is the profit motive which impels culture to spread its sway across the globe. The culture industry testifies less to the centrality of culture than to the expansionist ambitions of the late capitalist system, which can now colonise fantasy and enjoyment as intensively as it once colonised Kenya and the Philippines. In a curious irony, then, the larger mass culture looms, the more it appears as a phenomenon in its own right, but the less of an autonomous zone it actually is. Besides, the more influential this culture grows, the more it reinforces a global system whose ends are for the most part inimical to culture in the normative sense of the term.

The conventional postmodern wisdom is that this system has now taken a cultural turn. From the rough-spoken old industrial world, we have now evolved to capitalism with a cultural face. The role of the so-called 'creative' industries, the power of the new cultural technologies, the prominent role of sign, image, brand, icon, spectacle, lifestyle, fantasy, design and advertising: all this is taken to testify to the emergence of an 'aesthetic' form of capitalism, in transit from the material to the immaterial. What this amounts to, however, is that capitalism has incorporated culture for its own material ends, not that it has fallen under the sway of the aesthetic, gratuitous, self-delighting or self-fulfilling. On the contrary, this aestheticised mode of capitalist production has proved more ruthlessly instrumental than ever. 'Creativity', which for Marx and Morris signified the opposite of capitalist utility, is pressed into the service of acquisition and exploitation.

There is no clearer example of the way capitalism is intent on assimilating what once seemed its opposite ('culture') than the global decline of the universities. Along with the fall of Communism and the Twin Towers, it ranks among the most momentous events of our age, if somewhat less spectacular in nature. A centuries-old tradition of universities as centres of humane critique is currently being scuppered by their conversion into pseudo-capitalist enterprises under the sway of a brutally philistine managerial ideology. Once arenas of critical reflection, academic institutions are being increasingly reduced to organs of the marketplace, along with betting shops and fast food joints. They are now for the most part in the hands of technocrats for whom values are largely a matter of real estate. A new intellectual proletariat of academics is assessed by how far their lectures on Plato or Copernicus boost the economy, while unemployed graduates constitute a kind of lumpen intelligentsia. Students who are currently charged fees by the year will no doubt soon find their tutors charging by the insight. In moving some of its academic staff to new premises, one British university recently issued an edict severely restricting their ability to keep books in their minuscule offices. The idea of having a personal collection of books is becoming as archaic as Bill Haley or drainpipe trousers. The dream of our universities' boneheaded administrators is of a bookless and paperless environment, books and paper being messy, crumply stuff incompatible with a gleaming neo-capitalist wasteland consisting of nothing but machines, bureaucrats and security guards. Since students are also messy, crumply stuff, the ideal would be a campus on which no such inconvenient creatures were in sight. The death of the humanities is now an event waiting on the horizon.

What ought finally to have discredited the faith that capitalism has shifted to a new cultural mode was the financial debacle of 2008. One consequence of such upheavals is that, for an inconvenient moment, they strip the veil of familiarity from a form of life which has ceased to be regarded as a specific historical system. By throwing its inner workings into relief, they allow that life-form to be framed, objectified and

153

estranged. As such, it ceases to be the invisible colour of everyday life and can be seen instead as a historically recent mode of civilisation. Significantly, it is in the throes of such crises that even those who are supposed to run the system begin for the first time to use the word 'capitalism', rather than to speak more euphemistically of Western democracy or the Free World. They thus steal a march on some sectors of the cultural left, which in their zeal for a discourse of difference, diversity, identity and marginality ceased to use the word 'capitalism', let alone 'exploitation' or 'revolution', some decades ago. Neo-liberal capitalism has no difficulty with terms like 'diversity' or 'inclusiveness', as it does with the language of class struggle.

It is imprudent for the Masters of the Universe to talk of capitalism, since in doing so they acknowledge that their form of life is simply one among many, that like all other such life-forms it has a specific origin and that what was born can always die. It may be that capitalism is simply human nature, but it is hard to deny that there was a time when there was human nature but not capitalism. What the crisis of 2008 put most embarrassingly on show, however, was how little the system had fundamentally changed, for all the excited talk of lifestyle and hybridity, flexible identities and immaterial labour, rhizome-like organisations and open-necked CEO shirts, the disappearance of the working class and the shift from industrial labour to information technology and the service industry. Despite these innovations, the momentary crack-up of the system revealed that we were still languishing in a world of mass unemployment and obscenely overpaid executives, gross inequalities and squalid public services, one in which the state was every bit as obedient a tool of ruling-class interests as the most resolutely vulgar of Marxists had ever imagined. What was at stake was not image and icon but gargantuan fraud and systemic plunder. The true gangsters and anarchists wore pinstripe suits, and the robbers were running the banks rather than raiding them.

* * *

The idea of culture is traditionally bound up with the concept of distinction. High culture is a question of rank. One thinks of the great haut-bourgeois families portrayed by Marcel Proust and Thomas Mann, for whom power and material wealth are accompanied by a lofty cultural tone and bear with them certain moral obligations. Spiritual hierarchy goes hand in hand with social inequality. The aim of advanced capitalism, by contrast, is to preserve inequality while abolishing hierarchy. In this sense, its material base is at odds with its cultural superstructure. You do not need to proclaim your superiority to other peoples in order to raid their natural resources, as long as by doing so you maintain the material inequalities between them and yourself. Whether the Americans regard themselves as racially superior to the Iraqis is really neither here nor there, given that it is political and military control over an oil-rich region they have in their sights. Culturally speaking, late capitalism is for the most part a matter not of hierarchy but hybridity – of mingling, merging and multiplicity – while materially speaking the gulf between social classes assumes ultra-Victorian proportions. There are plenty of exponents of cultural studies who take note of the former but not the latter. While the sphere of consumption is hospitable to all comers, the domain of property and production remains rigidly stratified. Divisions of property and class, however, are partly masked by the levelling, demotic, spiritually promiscuous culture in which they are set, as they were not in the era of Proust and Mann. In contrast to that stately milieu, cultural and material capital now begin to split apart. The brokers, jobbers, shysters, operators and speculators who float to the top of the system in their spiritual weightlessness are hardly remarkable for their aesthetic wisdom.

The breaking down of cultural hierarchies is clearly to be welcomed. For the most part, however, it is less the upshot of a genuinely democratic spirit than an effect of the commodity form, which levels existing values rather than contesting them in the name of alternative priorities. Indeed, it represents an assault less on cultural supremacism than on the notion of value as such. The very act of discrimination becomes suspect. Not only does it involve exclusion, but it must inevitably imply the possibility of a superior vantage-point, which seems offensive to the egalitarian spirit. Those who prefer Billie Holliday to Liam Gallagher (and what right have they to judge in any case?) are simply being elitist. Since nothing is more common than evaluation in pubs and sports stadiums, this aversion to ranking is itself an elitist posture. Distinctions give way to differences. The cuisine of Florence, Arizona is neither better nor worse than that of Florence, Italy – simply different. To discriminate is unjustly to demean one thing while falsely absolutising another. To judge that Donald Trump has less humility than Pope Francis is to thrust Trump self-righteously into the outer darkness, thereby flouting the absolute value of inclusivity; and who am I to arrogate such authority? From what odiously Olympian standpoint has one the right to pontificate that feeding a gerbil is preferable to microwaving it?

The bogus populism of the commodity, its warm-hearted refusal to rank, exclude and discriminate, is based on a blank indifference to absolutely everyone. Careless for the most part of distinctions of class, race and gender, impeccably even-handed in its favours, it will yield itself, in the spirit of a whore-house, to anyone with the cash to buy it. A similar indifference underlies the historic advance of multiculturalism. If the human species now has a chance, for the first time in its history, to become thoroughly hybrid, it is largely because the capitalist market will buy the labour-power of anyone willing to sell it, whatever their cultural origins. There are, to be sure, some transitional tensions at work here. At present, it is the economy which is promiscuously open to all comers, and a certain current of racist culture which wishes to discriminate. A capitalist market accustomed to being culturally embedded in the nation-state, whose military firepower and social homogeneity served it well over the centuries, now pitches different ethnic groups together; and the racist and neo-fascist forces which this unleashes threatens to splinter the national cohesion on which a globalised economic system continues to depend. In this sense, mingling and multiplicity give birth to new forms of hierarchy and division.

For the moment, then, culture and the economy are in some sense out of synchrony. While the latter can go global, it is not so simple for the former to wax cosmopolitan. One can, to be sure, hang around polyglot cafés or enjoy the music of a score of nations, but culture in this sense of the term lacks the depth in which values and convictions need to be rooted. There are indeed international allegiances for which men and women have been ready to die, not least in the socialist tradition; but culture, as Burke was aware, draws much of its resilience from local loyalties. It is hard to imagine the citizens of Bradford or Bruges throwing themselves on the barricades crying 'Long live the European Union!' Far from producing citizens of the world, transnational capitalism tends to breed parochialism and insecurity among a large swathe of those subject to its sway; and it is towards racism and chauvinism, not into cosmopolitan cafés, that this insecurity is likely to impel them.

While some forms of culture have increased in significance, others have diminished. Nobody believes any longer that art can fill the shoes of the Almighty. Culture as a critique of civilisation has been increasingly eroded, undermined among other things by the postmodern prejudice that any such critique must address itself to an illusory social totality from an equally illusory standpoint of absolute knowledge. It has also come under siege, as we have seen, from the intellectual treason of the universities. The critical or utopian dimensions of the concept of culture are rapidly declining. If culture signifies a corporate way of life, as it does when we speak of deaf culture, beach culture, police culture, café culture and so on, then it is hard for it to serve at the same time as a yardstick by which to assess such forms of life, or to evaluate social existence in general. So-called identity politics are not remarkable for their self-critical spirit. The point of engaging in English folk culture is to affirm English folksiness, not to question it. Nobody becomes a Morris dancer in order to satirise the whole sorry business.

At the same time, there are political cultures (gay, feminist, ethnic, musical and so on) which are indeed deeply critical of the status quo. They inherit the dissenting impulse of *Kulturkritik* while jettisoning its spiritual elitism. They also reject its abstract utopianism for a specific way of life. If they challenge the patrician remoteness of the tradition which passes from Schiller to Lawrence, with its disdain for modernity, they also differ from those corporate life-forms which exist simply to affirm a particular social identity, rather than to cast a cold eye on the social order as a whole. Nobody but the most sorely misguided of citizens becomes a Morris dancer in order to overthrow capitalism, whereas many a feminist has greeted the prospect with acclaim. Political cultures of this kind combine critique with solidarity in something like the style of the traditional labour movement.

Yet though identity politics and multiculturalism can be radical forces, they are not for the most part revolutionary ones. Some of these political currents have largely abandoned their hopes in this regard, while others never entertained them in the first place. They differ in this respect from the powers which drove the British from India and the Belgians from the Congo. Those campaigns were quite properly a matter of expulsion and exclusion, not in the first place of plurality and inclusivity. They also envisaged a world beyond the horizon of capitalist reality, even if those visions were to be for the most part thwarted. Today's cultural politics, by contrast, is not generally given to challenging those priorities. It speaks the language of gender, identity, marginality, diversity and oppression, but not for the most part the idiom of state, property, class-struggle, ideology and exploitation. Roughly speaking, it is the difference between anti-colonialism and postcolonialism. Cultural politics of this kind are in one sense the very opposite of elitist notions of culture. Yet they share in their own way that elitism's overvaluing of cultural affairs, as well as its distance from the prospect of fundamental change.

What, finally, of the so-called war on terror? Is it not here that we should look for the persistence of cultural questions in political society? Perhaps one might see the collapse of the World Trade Center as a surreal explosion of archaic cultural forces at the very heart of modern civilisation. The clash between Western capitalism and radical Islam, however, is primarily a geopolitical affair, not a cultural or religious one, rather as the recent conflict in Northern Ireland had little to do with religious conviction. There has been much talk in the region of the need for an amicable encounter between what is blandly known as 'the two cultural traditions', Unionist and nationalist. It is thus that a history of injustice and inequality, of Protestant supremacy and Catholic subjugation, can be converted into an innocuous question of alternative cultural identities. Culture becomes a convenient way of displacing politics.

As in the case of revolutionary nationalism, culture may supply some of the terms on which material and political battles are joined, but it does not constitute their substance. By and large, fundamentalism is the creed of those who feel abandoned and humiliated by modernity, and the forces responsible for this pathological state of mind, like those which give birth to multiculturalism, are far from cultural in themselves. In fact, the central questions that confront a humanity moving into the new millennium are not cultural ones at all. They are far more mundane and material than that. War, hunger, drugs, arms, genocide, disease, ecological disaster: all of these have their cultural aspects, but culture is not the core of them. If those who speak of culture cannot do so without inflating the concept, it is perhaps better for them to remain silent.

Notes

1 Culture and Civilisation

1. Raymond Williams, *Keywords: A Vocabulary of Culture and Society* (revised edition, London: Fontana, 1983), p. 87.
2. Raymond Williams, *Culture and Society 1780–1950* (London: Chatto & Windus, 1958), p. 256.
3. T.S. Eliot, *Notes Towards the Definition of Culture* (London: Faber & Faber, 1948), p. 31.
4. Williams, *Culture and Society*, p. 234.
5. D.H. Lawrence, *Lady Chatterley's Lover*, quoted by Williams, *Culture and Society*, p. 201.
6. E.B. Tylor, *Primitive Culture*, vol. 1 (London: John Murray, 1871), p. 1.
7. Eliot, *Notes Towards the Definition of Culture*, p. 120.
8. Ibid., p. 27.
9. Ibid., p. 37.
10. Ibid., p. 19.
11. Slavoj Žižek, *Demanding the Impossible* (Cambridge: Polity Press, 2013), pp. 2, 9.
12. J.S. Mill, 'Coleridge' (1940), in F.R. Leavis (ed.), *Mill on Bentham and Coleridge* (Cambridge: Cambridge University Press, 1980), p. 56.
13. Henry James, letter to W.D. Howells, in Percy Lubbock (ed.), *Letters of Henry James*, vol. 1 (London: Macmillan, 1920), p. 72.

14. John Stuart Mill, *Dissertations and Discussions*, vol. 2 (London: Parker, 1859), p. 160.
15. Robert J.C. Young, *Colonial Desire* (London: Routledge, 1995), p. 53.
16. Sigmund Freud, *Civilisation and its Discontents*, ed. and trans. James Strachey (London: Hogarth Press, [1930] 1961), p. 89.

2 Postmodern Prejudices

1. A typical exponent of culturalism is the philosopher Richard Rorty. See in particular his *Philosophy and the Mirror of Nature* (Princeton, NJ: Princeton University Press, 1979) and *The Consequences of Pragmatism* (Minneapolis: University of Minnesota Press, 1982).
2. Friedrich Nietzsche, *On the Genealogy of Morals*, in Walter Kaufmann (ed.), *Basic Writings of Nietzsche* (New York: Random House, 1968), p. 498.

3 The Social Unconscious

1. Thomas W. Copeland (ed.), *The Correspondence of Edmund Burke* (Cambridge: Cambridge University Press, 1958), vol. 8, p. 378.
2. Quoted by Luke Gibbons, *Edmund Burke and Ireland* (Cambridge: Cambridge University Press, 2003), p. 121.
3. R.B. McDowell (ed.), *The Writings and Speeches of Edmund Burke* (Oxford: Clarendon Press, 1991), vol. 9, p. 644.
4. Quoted by Gibbons, *Edmund Burke and Ireland*, p. 124.
5. Ibid., p. 629.
6. Edmund Burke, *A Vindication of Natural Society* (Indianapolis: Liberty Fund, 1982), p. 88.
7. Edmund Burke, *The Works of the Right Honourable Edmund Burke*, ed. F.W. Rafferty (London: Oxford University Press, 1906–7), vol. 2, p. 184.
8. Ibid., p. 260.
9. McDowell (ed.), *Writings and Speeches of Edmund Burke*, vol. 9, p. 247.
10. *Works and Correspondence of the Right Honourable Edmund Burke* (London: Francis and John Rivington, 1852), vol. 5, p. 528.
11. Edmund Burke, *Reflections on the Revolution in France*, in *Select Works of Edmund Burke*, ed. Francis Canavan (Indianapolis: Liberty Fund, 1999), vol. 2, p. 194.
12. Quoted by Gibbons, *Edmund Burke and Ireland*, p. 121.
13. Ibid., p. 175.

14. Ibid.
15. Frederick G. Whelan, *Edmund Burke and India: Political Morality and Empire* (Pittsburgh: University of Pittsburgh Press, 1996), p. 5.
16. Quoted by Conor Cruise O'Brien, *The Great Melody* (London: Sinclair Stevenson, 1992), p. 311.
17. Quoted by Gibbons, *Edmund Burke and Ireland*, p. 175.
18. Edmund Burke, *The Works of the Right Honourable Edmund Burke* (London: George Bell and Sons, 1890), vol. 6, p. 465.
19. P.J. Marshall (ed.), *The Writings and Speeches of Edmund Burke* (Oxford: Clarendon Press, 1981), vol. 5, p. 402.
20. Quoted by O'Brien, *The Great Melody*, p. 324.
21. Paul Langford (ed.), *Writings and Speeches of Edmund Burke* (Oxford: Oxford University Press, 1981), vol. 2, p. 320.
22. Isaac Kramnick (ed.), *The Portable Burke* (Harmondsworth: Penguin, 1999), p. 520.
23. Burke, *Reflections on the Revolution in France*, p. 172.
24. Ibid., p. 170.
25. Ibid., pp. 152–3.
26. Ibid., p. 93.
27. Ibid., p. 192.
28. Ibid., p. 122.
29. Friedrich Schiller, *On the Aesthetic Education of Man*, ed. and trans. Elizabeth M. Wilkinson and L.A. Willoughby (Oxford: Clarendon Press, 1967), p. 37.
30. McDowell (ed.), *Writings and Speeches*, vol. 9, p. 479.
31. See Edmund Burke, *A Philosophical Enquiry into the Origin of our Ideas of the Sublime and Beautiful*, ed. J.T. Boulton (London: Routledge, 1958).
32. Ibid., p. 159.
33. David Hume, *Treatise of Human Nature* (Oxford: Oxford University Press, 1960), p. 556.
34. McDowell (ed.), *Writings and Speeches of Burke*, vol. 9, p. 614.
35. I have discussed this tradition more fully in my *Culture and the Death of God* (London: Yale University Press, 2014), ch. 6.
36. See A. Gillies, *Herder* (Oxford: Blackwell, 1945), p. 13.
37. Charles Taylor, *Philosophical Arguments* (Cambridge, MA: Harvard University Press, 1995), p. 79.
38. Quoted by Sonia Sikka, *Herder on Humanity and Cultural Difference* (Cambridge: Cambridge University Press, 2011), p. 17.

39. F.M. Barnard (ed.), *J.G. Herder on Social and Political Culture* (Cambridge: Cambridge University Press, 1969), p. 200.

40. J.G. Herder, *Another Philosophy of History and Selected Political Writings*, ed. and trans. Ioannis Evrigenis and David Pellerin (Indianapolis: Hackett, 2004), p. 100 (translation slightly modified).

41. For a judicious treatment of the subject, see Sonia Sikka's excellent study *Herder on Humanity and Cultural Difference*, ch. 4. See also John H. Zammito, *Kant, Herder, and the Birth of Anthropology* (Chicago: University of Chicago Press, 2002).

42. Barnard (ed.), *J.G. Herder*, p. 187.

43. Quoted by Robert J.C. Young, *Colonial Desire* (London: Routledge, 1995), p. 146.

44. Zammito, *Kant, Herder*, p. 333.

45. Quoted by Sikka, *Herder on Humanity*, p. 84.

46. See Terry Eagleton, *The Ideology of the Aesthetic* (Oxford: Blackwell, 1990), ch. 1.

47. T.S. Eliot, *Notes Towards the Definition of Culture* (London: Faber & Faber, 1948), p. 52.

48. T.W. Rolleston (ed.), *Thomas Davis: Selections from His Poetry and Prose* (Dublin: Talbot Press, 1920), p. 172.

49. Barnard (ed.), *J.G. Herder*, p. 203.

50. T.S. Eliot, *Notes towards the Definition of Culture*, p. 31.

51. Ibid., p. 94.

52. Ibid., pp. 106–7.

53. Ibid., p. 37.

54. Ibid., p. 35.

55. For a useful account of this tradition, see Francis Mulhern, *Culture/Metaculture* (London: Routledge, 2000).

56. Raymond Williams, *Culture and Society 1780–1950* (Harmondsworth: Penguin, 1958), p. 334.

57. Ibid., p. 238.

58. Ibid., p.335.

4 An Apostle of Culture

1. Richard Ellmann, *James Joyce* (Oxford: Oxford University Press, 1982), p. 226.

2. Oscar Wilde, 'The Soul of Man Under Socialism', in Terry Eagleton (ed.), *Oscar Wilde: Plays, Prose Writings and Poems* (London: Everyman, 1991).

3. Karl Marx, *Grundrisse* (Harmondsworth: Penguin, 1973), p. 488.
4. Karl Marx, *Capital* (New York: International Publishers, 1967), vol. 2, p. 820.
5. Wilde, 'The Soul of Man Under Socialism', in Eagleton (ed.), *Oscar Wilde*, p. 263.
6. Ibid., p. 283.

5 From Herder to Hollywood

1. Friedrich Schiller, *On the Aesthetic Education of Man*, trans. Elizabeth M. Wilkinson and L.A. Willoughby (Oxford: Clarendon Press, 1967), p. 35.
2. Ibid., p. 33.
3. Quoted by Raymond Williams, *Culture and Society 1780–1950* (Harmondsworth: Penguin, 1958), p. 201.
4. Schiller, *On the Aesthetic Education of Man*, p. 27.
5. Quoted by Williams, *Culture and Society*, p. 215.
6. The classic account of this lineage remains Raymond Williams's *Culture and Society*.
7. Lawrence E. Klein, *Shaftesbury and the Culture of Politeness* (Cambridge: Cambridge University Press, 1994), p. 11.
8. *Spectator*, no. 10, March 12th, 1711.
9. Schiller, *On the Aesthetic Education of Man*, p. 21.
10. Matthew Arnold, *Culture and Anarchy* (London: Macmillan, 1924), p. 56.
11. Ibid., p. 37.
12. Ibid., p. 199.
13. John Ruskin, *Stones of Venice* (London: George Allen, 1899), p. 165.
14. Quoted by Williams, *Culture and Society*, p. 139.
15. Ruskin, *Stones of Venice*, pp. 163ff.
16. Quoted by Williams, *Culture and Society*, p. 150.
17. Quoted in ibid., p. 154.
18. Elie Kedourie, *Nationalism* (London: Hutchinson, 1960), p. 70.
19. See Tom Kettle, *The Day's Burden* (Dublin: Browne and Nolan, 1937), p. 10.
20. I have developed this case more fully in 'Nationalism and the Case of Ireland', *New Left Review*, 234 (March/April 1999), pp. 44–61.
21. Robert J.C. Young, *Colonial Desire* (London: Routledge, 1995), p. 52.
22. Luke Gibbons, *Edmund Burke and Ireland* (Cambridge: Cambridge University Press, 2003), p. 174.

23. See Terry Eagleton, *Culture and the Death of God* (London: Yale University Press, 2014).

24. I.A. Richards, *Science and Poetry* (London: Kegan Paul, Trench, Trübner, 1926), pp. 82–3.

25. See Raymond Williams, *The Politics of Modernism* (London: Verso, 1989), p. 33.

26. F.R. Leavis, *Mass Civilisation and Minority Culture* (Cambridge: Minority Press, 1930), pp. 3–5.

27. Williams, *Culture and Society*, p. 257.

28. Ibid., p. 260.

Index